THE
AFRICAN-AMERICAN
ANSWER BOOK

The Ethnic Answer Books

The Ethnic Answer Books

THE
AFRICAN-AMERICAN
ANSWER BOOK

Ellen Shnidman

General Editors
Sandra Stotsky
Harvard Graduate School of Education
Reed Ueda
Tufts University

Chelsea House Publishers • Philadelphia

On the cover: *Aspects of Negro Life: From Slavery Through Reconstruction* (1934) by Aaron Douglas, oil on canvas; Art and Artifacts Division; Schomburg Center for Research in Black Culture; The New York Public Library; Astor, Lenox and Tilden Foundations

CHELSEA HOUSE PUBLISHERS

Editor in Chief: Stephen Reginald
Managing Editor: James D. Gallagher
Production Manager: Pamela Loos
Art Director: Sara Davis
Picture Editor: Judy L. Hasday
Senior Production Editor: Lisa Chippendale
Associate Art Director/Designer: Takeshi Takahashi
Picture Researcher: Lillian Mittleman

First Printing

1 3 5 7 9 8 6 4 2

The Chelsea House World Wide Web site address is
http://www.chelseahouse.com

Library of Congress Cataloging-in-Publication Data

Shnidman, Ellen.
The African-American answer book / Ellen Shnidman :
general editors, Sandra Stotsky, Reed Ueda.
   p. cm. — (The ethnic answer books)
Includes bibliographical references and index.
Summary: Presents questions covering the history, culture and social life, religion, political activities, economic life, and accomplishments of African-Americans, with a separate section for answers.

ISBN 0-7910-4912-4.
ISBN 0-7910-4913-2 (pbk.)

1. Afro-Americans—Miscellanea—Juvenile literature. 2. Questions and answers—Juvenile literature. [1. Afro-Americans—Miscellanea. 2. Questions and answers.] I. Stotsky, Sandra. II. Ueda, Reed. III. Title.IV. Series: Shnidman, Ellen. Ethnic Answer books.
E185.S46 1998
973'0496-73'0076—dc21   98-16323
                                                                           CIP
                                                                           AC

CONTENTS

Introduction
ETHNIC ANSWER BOOKS

Over half a century ago, Louis Adamic, a Slovenian immigrant who had become a popular writer, described the United States as a country "all of a piece, a blend of cultures from many lands, woven of threads from many corners of the world." The history of the United States shows that this nation has indeed been woven from many strands. More immigrants and more ethnic groups have come to live in America than in any other country in the world. In fact, the United States has been the most powerful magnet for international migration in world history.

Extensive immigration began in the 17th century when English settlers began to colonize North America, intermingling with the early Dutch settlers as well as the indigenous peoples of this continent. Blacks also came in large numbers, imported from Africa to serve as slaves. Well before the American Revolution, other groups of people—the Germans, French Huguenots, Scots, Welsh, and Scotch-Irish were the major groups—also began to migrate here. After the American Revolution, the United States' favorable immigration policies led to a large influx of immigrants, who helped settle and develop the new country. From 1820 to 1930, 38,000,000 people moved to the United States while 24,000,000 people migrated to Canada, Argentina, Brazil, Australia, New Zealand, South Africa, and other areas. From World War II to the early 1990s, 20,000,000 newcomers flocked to the United States. As a result of these continuous waves of migration to America's shores, the United States and Canada have evolved into multi-ethnic countries of remarkable proportions, with each having absorbed an enormous variety of ethnic groups.

Educators at all levels are now encouraging greater attention to the many dimensions of American diversity, especially our religious and ethnic diversity. As a part of their study of American history, students are now being asked to learn about the Irish, Italians, Chinese, Poles, Mexicans, and Germans—to name some of our country's major immigrant ethnic groups—as well as the African Americans and the indigenous peoples of this continent. Indeed, the distinctive characteristics and contributions of all this country's ethnic groups have now taken a place at the center of our school curriculum.

This new series of educational texts seeks to provide secondary students with a handy and compact reference work they can use to learn how a democratic nation was built out of intermixture and interdependence. All the volumes in this series are similar in three important respects. Every volume has a question and answer format. Each book supplies a core of factual information about a particular ethnic group. And all the volumes are organized by common chapters.

The creators of this series have designed this format to accomplish several educational goals. First, we offer questions about key features of the group's life and history in order to arouse students' curiosity about this particular group of Americans. Questions also serve to provide models of inquiry for students; these are the kinds of questions a historian asks when seeking to understand the history and life of a group of people. Second, the answers we provide to these questions are designed to yield a nucleus of significant facts. These facts can be drawn on for research reports, and they can serve as a point of departure for further inquiry into the history and experiences of an ethnic group. Finally, all the questions are organized into common chapters across all books in the series so that students can make informative comparisons and contrasts among American ethnic groups.

The first two chapters in each volume deal with the group's origins and arrival in America. The next three chapters provide information on the group's economic, religious, and social life and institutions in this country. Another three chapters present information on the group's distinctive characteristics, intellectual and cultural life, and participation in American public life. The final chapter describes important or accomplished individuals in this group's history in America. By comparing and contrasting information in these chapters among various ethnic groups, students have an excellent opportunity to learn about many significant features of American life, both in the past and today. They can learn about the different ways that each group has drawn on America's political principles and institutions to integrate its members into American political life. They can discover the different ways that America's ethnic groups interacted with each other as well as with the descendants of the English settlers who framed this country's political principles and institutions. They can find out how members of each group took advantage of this country's free public schools and free public libraries to advance themselves socially, intellectually, and economically. And students can begin to understand the remarkable similarities in the experiences of many ethnic groups in this country despite their having come from many different parts of the world, as well as the remarkable differences among ethnic groups who have come from the same parts of the world.

It is our hope that this series of books will serve as an intellectual guidepost to further student learning. It will help supply a solid foundation of knowledge that students can draw on to supplement what they learn in their classes on American history, literature, and government. And students will learn how to ask "good" questions about ethnicity. They will learn from the answers that it is a subject full of surprises and complexity—that ethnicity is not equivalent to race or language, that an ethnic group's characteristics depend heavily on when large numbers of its members arrive in this country, and that a group's characteristics change markedly from generation to generation in America. As a result, students will find the study of ethnic history a fascinating experience of discovery about how this country became the most successful democracy in history.

—Sandra Stotsky and Reed Ueda

Foreword
THE AFRICAN AMERICANS

O f all the people who have come to America in the last 400 years, no group has a more tragic history than African Americans. At the same time, no other group has made as much progress in such a short time as have black Americans in the last 60 years. The first Africans came to America in 1619. They were servants for the early English settlers of colonial Virginia. But for the next 200 years, Africans came to America from the coast of West Africa on slave ships bound mainly for southern colonies and states.

From 1620 until 1865 most African Americans lived as slaves in the southern part of the United States. About 10 percent of the black population had been freed (or had escaped) from slavery before President Lincoln issued the Emancipation Proclamation during the Civil War. Under slavery, blacks were kept illiterate and were prevented from developing normal community institutions.

After the Civil War, African Americans faced the huge task of rebuilding their families, creating community institutions, and making themselves a part of the emerging industrial society in America. Despite their great poverty, they were able to build churches, colleges, schools and neighborhoods.

The great majority of blacks lived in the South until the 20th century. During the 20th century, a large number of southern blacks moved to cities in the North and West. This move transformed them into a literate, mostly urban population. About half of them remained in the South. The other half settled in the rest of the country. A great flowering of black culture has occurred as a result.

From the 1920s until today, few groups have contributed as much as African Americans to forming a distinctly American culture. Most of the identifiably American forms of music created in the 20th century were partly or fully the result of black influence—from ragtime to rock 'n' roll to rap. Many of America's most important writers in this century have been black. Their writing reflects the unique struggles and perspectives of blacks in America.

The black influence in contemporary pop culture is huge—whether reflected in television, in movies, or in sports. The great accomplishments of the American sports world are in large part due to black athletes. They make up a disproportionate share of professional and Olympic athletes.

All of these achievements, however, are the fruit of a 100-year struggle for civil rights and equal opportunity in this society. Although the Civil War emancipated four million black slaves, the gates of opportunity didn't begin to open for the freed slaves and their descendants until World War II. Jim Crow laws in the South and discrimination in the North blocked upward mobility for blacks for many generations.

During World War II, opportunities in the defense industry opened up for black workers. These jobs gave them new skills and raised their incomes. The average number of years black children attended school and the proportion of black adults with college educations rose dramatically from 1940 until the 1980s. During these years there was a large increase in the size of the black middle class. These economic and educational achievements were partly a result of the civil rights movement.

Black activists and sympathetic whites had been working for civil rights for African Americans since the abolition movement in the early 19th century. However, it wasn't until the 1950s and 1960s that civil rights laws and equal opportunity guarantees for black citizens were passed and enforced. The Rev. Martin Luther King Jr., a person of unique vision, oratorical skill, and moral authority, provided leadership to the movement such as had not been seen since the days of Frederick Douglass in the mid-19th century.

Since the 1960s the black community has experienced a growing split. In the days of legal segregation, few blacks were well off, and most lived in the same neighborhoods or in rural areas of the South. Now other choices exist. A black middle and upper middle class has moved into its own neighborhoods or into integrated suburbs. Low-income blacks, who live on public assistance, remain concentrated in inner cities or in the small-town South. The interests of these two groups are no longer the same, as they were during the struggle for basic civil rights. Moreover, no leader of the stature of Martin Luther King Jr. has become a source of authority for the more than 30 million African Americans.

The challenge for the black community is how to use the success and wealth of its middle class to renew the part of its population living in decaying inner cities. This requires strategies different from those of the civil rights era. It also will need the cooperation and good will of the broader society.

New groups have arisen within the black community in the past 20 years. They stress the importance of economic enterprise in the inner city, individual responsibility, and higher standards in education. Some of the original civil rights organizations such as the NAACP and the Urban League are revising their agendas to deal with current challenges. Whether these groups can assist the bottom third of the black population or whether this underclass will be manipulated by political opportunists remains an unresolved question.

—Ellen Shnidman

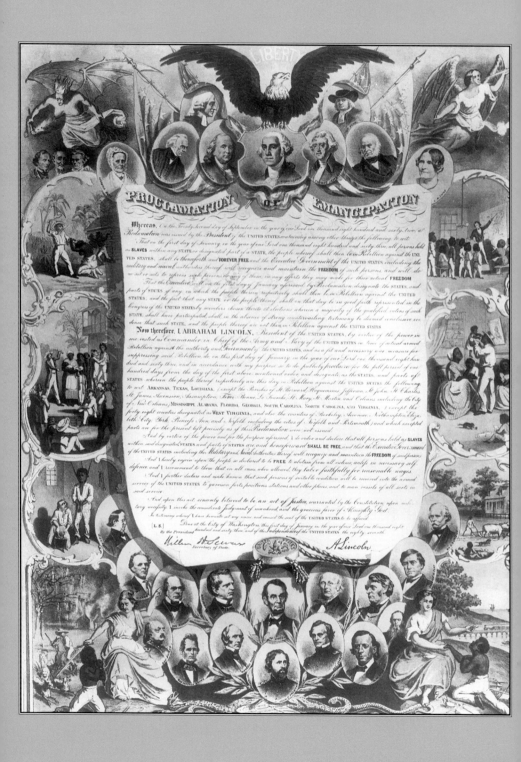

Questions

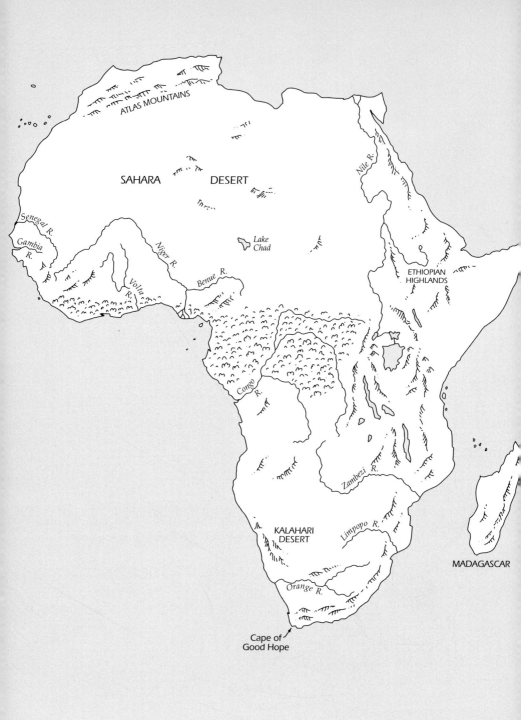

ATLAS MOUNTAINS

SAHARA DESERT

Senegal R.

Gambia R.

Niger R.

Volta R.

Benue R.

Lake Chad

Nile R.

ETHIOPIAN HIGHLANDS

Congo R.

Zambezi R.

Limpopo R.

KALAHARI DESERT

Orange R.

Cape of Good Hope

MADAGASCAR

◀ Because Africa, the second largest continent, is transversed by the equator, its climate is predominantly tropical. A large percentage of its inhabitants live in hot, wet areas. The continent comprises 22 percent of the world's land area and approximately 11 percent of its population.

CHAPTER

1

ORIGINS

Life in Early Africa

1-1 From what region of Africa did the ancestors of most of today's African Americans come?

1-2 What forms of religion did the Africans originally follow before their exposure to Islam and Christianity?

1-3 What was one of the central beliefs about family life in African religion?

1-4 What forms of social organization did Africans have?

1-5 As in all areas of life, the extended family or clan was the focus for African religious life. Who served the priestly functions in this form of religion?

1-6 What made up a typical African clan?

1-7 The ancient kingdom of Ghana, which occupied a large part of West Africa, was the first great black African kingdom. It was probably organized in the seventh century. What prompted Africans to establish political entities larger than the traditional extended family?

1-8   By the 10th century, the kingdom of Ghana became known for its production and sale of what resource?

1-9   What African kingdom surpassed the kingdom of Ghana in size and might by the 14th century?

1-10   The greatest of all African kingdoms reached its peak in the 15th century. Which kingdom (or empire) was this?

1-11   What was the major reason for African rulers to expand their dominion over larger pieces of territory?

1-12   How did the size of the great West African empires compare to those in Europe during the 11th through 15th centuries?

Africa During the Period of Muslim and European Contacts

1-13   When did Islam spread to black West Africa?

1-14   What were some of the reasons the elite classes of West Africa converted to Islam?

1-15   The institution of slavery was practiced in Africa, as it was almost everywhere in the ancient world. What were the distinguishing characteristics of African slavery?

1-16   What outside force transformed local African slavery into a form of international commerce?

1-17   Since slavery contradicts the teachings of Islam, how did Arab Muslims justify their involvement in it?

1-18   What new use for slaves did Europeans have when they became involved in the slave trade in the 16th century?

1-19 Since slavery contradicts the teachings of Christianity, how did European Christians justify their involvement in it?

1-20

What European country got involved in the African slave trade first?

1-21

What were the two commodities that the Africans traded to the Portuguese?

1-22

How did European merchants acquire slaves?

1-23

Who replaced the Portuguese as the major European slave traders? When did this happen?

1-24

What three-way economic transaction was involved in the slave trade?

1-25

Why did the British finally outlaw the transatlantic slave trade?

1-26

How long did the Muslim-dominated slave trade to the Near East continue?

1-27

How many slaves are estimated to have been part of the transatlantic slave trade and the slave trade to the Middle East?

The West Indies

1-28

What was the main reason slaves were taken to the West Indies?

1-29

Haiti is a unique country in the West Indies because of the way in which it was founded. How did it become an independent country?

1-30

When was slavery outlawed in Haiti?

▲ African-American soldiers, like these members of the Ninth U.S. Cavalry, were given the distinguishing nickname "Buffalo Soldiers" by Native Americans in the western territories. Regiments of black soldiers had served in the U.S. Army during the Civil War, and in 1867 Congress approved the creation of all-black infantry and cavalry regiments. Between 1867 and 1890, the Ninth and Tenth U.S. Cavalry regiments gained a reputation as excellent fighting units.

CHAPTER

2

ARRIVAL IN AMERICA

The Slave Trade and the South

2-1 How many African slaves came to America?

2-2 Were there attempts to enslave people other than Africans?

2-3 What percentage of slaves taken in Africa died during the trip across the ocean?

2-4 What were the major causes of death in the slave population?

2-5 What was "chattel slavery"?

2-6 In what area of the country did most slaves live when they reached America?

2-7 Why did so few slaves live in the other region?

2-8 When did Congress abolish the slave trade?

2-9 Even after the slave trade was abolished in 1807, the slave population in the South continued to increase. What was the reason for this?

Black Migration to the North and West

2-10 Who were the "buffalo soldiers?"

2-11 What does the phrase "the great migration" refer to when applied to African Americans in the 20th century?

2-12 The great migration produced a lasting change in where African Americans lived. Explain what the change was and why it happened.

2-13 How did the great migration change northern cities?

2-14 What was the reaction of whites when blacks began moving to the cities during and after World War I?

2-15 What is Harlem?

2-16 How did the pattern of where African Americans were living change during the mid-1980s?

2-17 What were some of the factors that caused this change?

2-18 What did the Fair Housing Act of 1968 set out to accomplish?

2-19 What change in where African Americans live has occurred in the past 30 years, partly as a result of the Fair Housing Act?

2-20 What are some of the reasons for this change in where African Americans choose to live?

Immigration from the West Indies and Africa

2-21 Immigrants from the West Indies have been coming to America since the early 20th century. When did the number of these immigrants become significant?

2-22 What caused a wave of immigration from Haiti after 1965?

2-23 Since 1965, the majority of Haitian and Dominican immigrants have settled in one urban area. Which area is this?

2-24 Haitian immigrants have tended not to mix much with African Americans. What are the reasons for this?

2-25 Blacks from the British-controlled islands of the West Indies began to migrate to American cities in the early 20th century. What distinguished these immigrants from other immigrants of that period and from rural southern blacks?

2-26 In the last 20 years or so, small numbers of Nigerians, Ghanians, Ethiopians, Eritreans, and Somalis have immigrated to the United States from Africa. What are the reasons for their immigration?

◀ Although only 25 percent of the southern population owned slaves, there were nearly four million slaves in the South by 1860. Almost half of these slaves were used strictly for planting and harvesting the five million bales of cotton produced on southern plantations each year.

CHAPTER

3

ECONOMIC LIFE

The Plantation System

3-1 What characteristics of the New World lent themselves to the introduction of slave labor?

3-2 By the late 18th century, the institution of slavery was under attack by abolitionists, especially in the North. What caused the need for slaves to increase during the 1790s?

3-3 On the eve of the Civil War, the economy of the South was largely based on one crop. What was it? Where was it sold?

3-4 What percentage of slaves were involved in producing cotton?

3-5 Why did most slave masters keep their slaves illiterate?

The Post-Slavery South

3-6 After the Civil War ended in 1865, former slaves were freed, but their economic situation didn't change much. Why was this the case?

3-7 The movement of blacks from rural areas to southern cities, and later to northern cities, began during and after the Civil War. What pushed southern blacks off the land and into the cities?

3-8 After the Civil War, numerous fraternal and self-help organizations sprang up among blacks living in the South. Which service industry established in Durham, North Carolina, in the late 1800s grew out of a mutual aid society and became a major African-American enterprise in the 20th century?

3-9 A black-run life insurance industry was created because of racial prejudice. Explain how this was so.

Urban Life

3-10 Although blacks in the North after the Civil War were in a better situation than those in the South, they faced many problems. They did not have as many economic opportunities as people immigrating from Europe at the same time. What were some of the unique obstacles blacks experienced?

3-11 Two black labor unions were established in 1869. They were distinct from the National Labor Union, the first American labor union, which was established in 1866. Why did black workers feel it was necessary to establish their own union?

3-12 The most important trade union in America, the American Federation of Labor (AFL), was founded in 1881. However, at first even the AFL refused to demand the inclusion of black workers in local unions. Why was this so?

3-13 During the 1930s, which national labor union took the lead in trying to integrate black workers into the unionized work force?

3-14 Walter Reuther, the president of the United Auto Workers Union (1949–1970), made this union into one of the most powerful and progressive of all the labor unions. What important contribution did he make in the field of race relations?

3-15 In 1955, the Congress of Industrial Organizations (CIO) merged with the AFL, producing the biggest union of American workers. Which black man was elected as one of the vice presidents of this union?

3-16 What change in the status of black workers was symbolized by African-American labor leaders taking top positions in the AFL-CIO in the 1950s?

3-17 As World War II began, the growing defense industry produced high paying jobs for blue-collar workers. Initially, blacks were shut out of these jobs. What action did they take to change this situation? Why was the change an important turning point for African Americans in industry and government?

3-18 Employment during World War II led to great gains for African Americans after the war. What were these gains?

3-19 The black middle class made enormous gains from 1950 to the present day. In 1950 only 5 percent of black workers were professionals or managers. What is the percentage today?

3-20 The huge growth of the black middle class beginning in the 1960s was partly a result of the affirmative action policies of the 1960s and '70s. What were affirmative action policies supposed to achieve?

3-21 While affirmative action policies were at first seen by most Americans as just compensation for years of discrimination against minorities, that is no longer the case. What are current attitudes on this issue?

3-22 What former factory worker in Detroit borrowed $800 and started one of the most successful record companies of the 1960s?

3-23 In the 1960s, Stokely Carmichael coined the phrase "Black Power." To what was he referring?

3-24 *Fortune* magazine, an important American business magazine, had a cover story in August 1997 entitled "The New Black Power." To what was it referring?

3-25 *Fortune* magazine cites the statistic that in 1973 the top 100 black-owned businesses had revenues of $470,000. What was the revenue of the top 100 in 1996?

3-26 Roughly 30 percent of the black population in America still lives in poverty, a number that has remained the same for the past 20 years. What are some of the reasons for the persistence of this poverty?

3-27 How is the black population of the borough of Queens in New York City unique?

3-28 Why has the U.S. military been such a successful vehicle for upward mobility and integration of the working-class black population?

3-29 What strategies are black community leaders employing in the 1990s to gain support for urban renewal?

3-30 What are some current examples of urban renewal led by black civic leaders?

The South's Slave Economy

By 1860, just before the start of the Civil War, African-American slaves worked to produce many kinds of products, including tobacco in the Mid-Atlantic states, lumber in some southeastern states, rice in the Carolinas, and sugar cane in parts of Florida and Louisiana. However, cotton superseded all of these as the primary occupation for slave labor.

Cotton had been a relatively unprofitable crop before 1793 and the invention of the cotton gin, for many reasons. It required an enormous amount of time and expensive, exhausting manual labor—hence the need for such a large workforce of slaves. Because cotton drains the soil of nutrients, the crop could not be planted on the same field continually. Thus, planters had to own vast amounts of land to have a profitable cotton crop. In the southeastern states in particular, unpredictable weather and pests like the boll weevil could wipe out entire crops (and still do). In 1793, the cotton gin cut down on the time and effort spent in manufacturing fabric, and harvested by an enslaved human labor force, cotton made southern plantations extremely profitable for decades. However, the gin could not solve the inherent problems with the cotton crop. By the 1860s, most of the southeastern United States was suffering from soil exhaustion because of heavy cotton production. ■

◀ Martin Luther King Jr. (1929-68) and Malcolm X (1925-65) were two of the most important leaders of the civil rights movement in the 1960s. Although they were working toward the same goal—equal rights for African Americans—their methods differed widely. Dr. King stressed peaceful solutions and passive resistance, while Malcolm X originally advocated a violent black revolution, although he later denounced violence as a solution. Both men were assassinated in the late 1960s, and blacks and whites all over the world mourned the loss of two great leaders.

CHAPTER

4

RELIGIOUS LIFE

The Old South and Christianity

4-1 When did large numbers of slaves begin to convert to Christianity?

4-2 During slavery, black religious life was controlled and manipulated by the plantation owners. What did they do?

4-3 One of the best known spirituals is "Nobody Knows the Trouble I've Seen." What are the lyrics to this song, and what do they mean?

4-4 What are some well-known images from spirituals?

4-5 Why were the themes of the Old Testament so popular among black slaves?

The Growth of Black Churches

4-6 The first black churches were established in the late 18th and early 19th centuries. The African Methodist Episcopal Church and the Negro Baptist Church were theologically similar to their white counterparts. Why were separate black churches established?

4-7   The chanted sermon is characteristic of the preaching style of many black ministers. What are some of the qualities of the chanted sermon?

4-8   What non-religious role did black churches play over the last two centuries?

4-9   The Ebenezer Baptist Church in Atlanta was founded in the 1880s. What is this church famous for?

4-10   What important and lasting role have black churches played in African American political life?

Recent Trends

4-11   The vast majority of black Americans (close to 100 percent) became Protestants during slavery. After the great migration in the 20th century, they were exposed to other forms of American-derived religious life in northern cities. What were these other religions?

4-12   What impact did exposure to other types of religion have on black religious life?

4-13   Recent black immigrants from Haiti and Cuba have brought certain African-derived forms of religion that never died out in the Caribbean. What are these?

4-14   What is Rastafarianism?

4-15   What background do most Rastafarians have?

4-16   What qualities have attracted blacks from inner-city neighborhoods to religious sects like Catholicism, the Black Muslims, traditional Judaism, Jehovah's Witnesses, and Baptists?

4-17 How has the Catholic Church expanded its influence on African Americans in northern cities?

4-18 Why do so many black parents in northern cities choose to send their children to Catholic schools, even though most of them are Protestant?

4-19 The original Black Muslim movement began in Detroit, Michigan, in the 1930s. Who founded the movement?

4-20 How did this movement's philosophy change over time?

4-21 What percentage of the original African slaves were probably followers of Islam?

4-22 Malcolm X originally adhered to and promoted the separatist views of Elijah Muhammad. Before he was assassinated, he had a change of heart. What caused him to change his mind?

▲ Born into slavery in 1856, Booker T. Washington (1856–1915) rose to become one of America's most important black leaders, and his work opened the door to black progress in America. In 1881 he founded the Tuskegee Institute, a school that helped blacks learn a trade and work toward a degree, in Alabama. His famous Atlanta Compromise address of 1895 was met with mixed acceptance among blacks. Some African Americans admired Washington's desire to uplift their race, but others were critical of his reluctance to push for immediate civil rights.

CHAPTER

5

SOCIAL LIFE AND INSTITUTIONS

Plantation Life and Slavery

5-1 What impact did slavery have on the structure of the black family?

5-2 Who was Nat Turner? Why did he become famous?

5-3 Plantation slaves held different positions of social status. What created those differences?

5-4 In 1780 Pennsylvania became the first state to abolish slavery. Why did this happen?

5-5 In 1817 the American Colonization Society was founded by a varied collection of white groups and individuals. What was the purpose of this society?

5-6 What were the main motives of the groups who supported the colonization scheme?

5-7 Why did the colonization movement fade away before the Civil War?

5-8 What was the Underground Railroad?

5-9 The militant phase of the antislavery or abolition movement began in the 1830s. What ideas motivated people to support the antislavery movement?

5-10 Who were the people most prominent in the antislavery movement before the Civil War?

5-11 Why was Frederick Douglass an important figure in the abolition movement?

5-12 When did President Lincoln issue a directive to free the slaves in the South?

The South After the Civil War

5-13 One of the first black leaders to realize that more than political action was needed to improve the lives of freed slaves was Booker T. Washington. What was his approach to the problem of black poverty, and what did he do about it?

5-14 One of the most prestigious black colleges in America was founded in 1882. What is the name of this college, and where was it founded?

5-15 From the end of the Civil War until World War I (1865–

1914) both blacks and whites worked to establish schools and colleges for recently freed slaves. In 1854 there was only one black college. How many were there by the middle of the 20th century?

5-16 The Ku Klux Klan was founded after the Civil War in 1866. It flourished during the bitterness of the Reconstruction period but then began to fade. When was it revived, and how did it change?

City Life

5-17 In the late 19th and early 20th centuries, several black leaders tried to launch "Back to Africa" movements. Name the two prominent leaders associated with this idea.

5-18 During the years when blacks began to move in huge numbers to cities, many biracial organizations were established to provide aid for them. Name some of these groups.

5-19 "The Negro race, like all races, is going to be saved by its exceptional men." Who made this comment, and to what was he referring?

5-20 Organizations like the NAACP in the early part of the century were not able to lead African Americans as well as they would have liked. Why was this?

5-21 What accounted for the large number of African Americans who followed Marcus Garvey in the 1920s?

5-22 What was the long-term significance of Garvey's version of a "Back to Africa" movement, or "Negro Zionism" as it was called?

5-23 During the great migration, black extended families were disrupted, and the overcrowded, dehumanizing conditions of urban slums took a further toll on the family. What other factors had a damaging impact on the stability of black family life in northern cities?

Post-World War II America

5-24 Many of the negative attitudes of other Americans toward integration of blacks into American society changed as a result of World War II. What happened during that time to cause people to reevaluate their views of racial integration?

5-25 In 1950 the United States Army was officially desegregated. It has became a major path of upward mobility for working-class blacks. What brought about this change in policy?

5-26 In the 1960s a number of prominent black militants revived the idea of a "Back to Africa" movement. They were partly inspired by the decolonization process that had recently led to the creation of dozens of independent African states. Who were the militants who returned to Africa, and what happened to them?

5-27 In the mid-1960s, a number of young blacks who had been active in the civil rights movement founded an organization called the Black Panthers. From the mid-1960s to the early 1970s, the Black Panthers gained a certain amount of support in low-income black neighborhoods. Why did they attract this support?

5-28 What brought about the end of the Black Panthers?

5-29 A focus on self-help and self-reliance instead of racial integration was conceived by Booker T. Washington at the turn of this century. What other black leaders have held similar views since then?

5-30 In what ways does the appeal of Louis Farrakhan seem similar to that of Marcus Garvey?

5-31 In what other respects is the support for Farrakhan similar to that for Garvey?

5-32 In 1981 a black organization called Transafrica Forum was founded. What was its purpose?

NAACP

JOIN!
GIVE!

NATIONWIDE MEMBERSHIP DRIVE

1909

NATIONAL ASSOCIATION FOR THE
ADVANCEMENT OF COLORED PEOPLE
20 WEST 40th STREET NEW YORK 18, N.Y.

1949

◀ The National Association for the Advancement of Colored People, or NAACP, was founded in 1909, making it the oldest and largest civil-rights group today. Through posters such as this one from 50 years ago, the group urged African Americans to donate their time and money to help achieve their goal—the "elimination of all barriers to political, educational, social, and economic equality."

CHAPTER

6

GROUP CHARACTERISTICS

Demographic Data

6-1 Before the Emancipation Proclamation, how many black slaves lived in the United States?

6-2 There were also free blacks in the United States before slavery was outlawed. How many free blacks lived in America at that time?

6-3 How did the free blacks obtain their freedom?

6-4 After the Civil War and into the 20th century, African Americans made up the majority of the population in three southern states. What were these three states?

6-5 In 1910, 10 million blacks lived in the United States. Ninety percent of them lived in the South. By 1980, the black population in America had reached 25 million. What percent of this population lived in the South?

6-6 What is the black population in America today?

6-7 In the early 19th century, the literacy rate among blacks was less than 10 percent. What was the literacy rate by the early 20th century?

6-8 Before World War II, most black students went to historically black colleges. What trend in college education began in the 1960s?

6-9 The black population in America today is made up of at least four important ethnic subgroups. What are they?

6-10 From the Civil War until the 1960s, African Americans were the only nonwhite population of any significant size in the country. (Native Americans had a small population and lived mostly on reservations, where they were not very visible. The Asian population was also small, and it was concentrated in California and Hawaii.) How has this situation changed in the last 30 years?

Class and Social Divisions

6-11 During the last century, debate over a strategy for improving the lives of African Americans has divided black intellectuals. What were the two main views on this issue?

6-12 Why did the leadership of the black community after the Civil War come mostly from those who had been freed before the Civil War?

6-13 Henry Louis Gates Jr., a leading black intellectual, has said that this is the best of times and worst of times for blacks in America. What does he mean by that?

6-14 What is the main difference between opinions in the black community about the issue of integration?

Cultural Subgroups

6-15 Some historians categorize the emerging African-American culture of the 18th and 19th centuries into three subcultures based on regional differences. What regions produced these three subcultures?

6-16 What events have occurred during the 20th century to blur the differences between these regional subcultures?

6-17 What broad cultural changes occurred when many blacks moved to cities in the 20th century?

6-18 What makes the African-American culture that emerged in the early 20th century different from the traditional African culture of the original slaves?

6-19 In the last 30 years many black American families have begun to celebrate a holiday called Kwanzaa. What does this holiday celebrate?

6-20 Why and how was the holiday of Kwanzaa created?

6-21 A disproportionate share of black American community leaders and intellectuals in the 20th century came from a British West Indian background. Name some of them.

6-22 Why did the British West Indies produce such an accomplished black educated class in the 20th century?

◀ Thelonious Monk (1917-1982) was a jazz composer and pianist whose work was largely overlooked until the 1950s. In 1957 he appeared in the television program *The Sound of Jazz,* and he later played at many well-known music halls, including New York's Town Hall, Carnegie Hall, and Lincoln Center. Monk's talent and innovation in the field made him an inspiration for future generations of African-American musicians like Herbie Hancock, who is standing next to Monk at the piano.

CHAPTER

7

CULTURAL LIFE

Music

7-1 The traveling minstrel show was a uniquely black form of entertainment that originated in the South. What popular American forms of dance evolved out of the minstrel show?

7-2 Most of the distinctively American forms of music in the 20th century originally came from black music. Give examples of five types of American music that are either mostly or entirely black forms of music.

7-3 Ragtime music was invented around the turn of the 20th century by southern black musicians. It had a short burst of popularity and then disappeared. How has it been revived in the last 20 years?

7-4 Who was the most famous composer and performer of ragtime music?

7-5 What was the musical origin of ragtime, and how was its most famous composer introduced to it?

7-6   Jazz music was created by the merging of three earlier forms of music. What were these forms of music?

7-7   Jazz continued to develop after World War II. Name some of its most accomplished performers.

7-8   Who is the jazz pianist best known as the leader of a popular Big Band-era "orchestra?"

7-9   The Marsalis family from New Orleans produced many accomplished musicians. Who are the musical members of this family?

7-10   Rock 'n' roll music developed in the 1950s and '60s. It originated primarily from British and African-American influences. Who are the black musicians considered among the originators of rock 'n' roll?

7-11   The most successful black-owned record company was Motown, which was based in Detroit. What was the key to Motown's success?

7-12   Name five of the most successful Motown performers or groups from the 1950s and '60s.

7-13   One of the greatest female vocalists of the 1960s was the daughter of a black Baptist minister in Detroit. Who was this "Queen of Soul"?

7-14   In what kind of music have Leontyne Price, Kathleen Battle, and Jessye Norman—all black women—excelled?

7-15   What is the origin of reggae music, and how was it introduced to American audiences?

Writers

7-16   Who is considered the first African-American writer in

American history, and what made her unique as a writer and as a black woman of that period?

7-17 Who is considered the second major American black writer and what was distinctive about his style of writing?

7-18 Name five major African-American writers in the 20th century.

7-19 After World War I the number of black newspapers and magazines increased steadily. By 1979, 350 black journals regularly covered aspects of black life not well covered by the mainstream press. What are some of the best known of these journals?

7-20 In the 1920s accomplished white playwrights such as Eugene O'Neill began to write plays dealing with African-American life. This offered opportunities in the theater for talented black actors. Which famous black actor got his start in these dramas?

7-21 Harlem became a magnet for black artists, musicians, and writers in the 1920s. By then it had become the largest black urban neighborhood in the nation, with 200,000 people. During this decade there was an outpouring of cultural creativity. What was the name given to this phenomenon?

7-22 The black writers of the 1920s were determined to change the portrayal of blacks in the broader American culture. What sort of change did they envision?

7-23 James Weldon Johnson was one of the most brilliant figures of the Harlem Renaissance. What is considered his most important contribution to this movement?

7-24 Who is considered the greatest poet of the Harlem Renaissance period?

7-25 Langston Hughes wrote many poems that became very famous and are often quoted. What was probably his most famous poem?

7-26 The phrase "raisin in the sun" was used as the name for an award-winning play. Who wrote it?

7-27 Who were the two most acclaimed black writers of the immediate post–World War II period? What characterized their writing?

7-28 In the 1970s, an African American named Alex Haley wrote a book called *Roots.* It was later made into a popular television miniseries. What was the theme of *Roots?*

7-29 The story of *Roots* ignited a social phenomenon among black Americans and Americans of other ethnic backgrounds as well. What phenomenon was this?

7-30 Some of the best contemporary black writers are women. Name three of the best known.

7-31 "I know why the caged bird sings" is a line in a well-known poem by a black poet. Who was the poet, and what was the poem?

7-32 *I Know Why the Caged Bird Sings* is also the name of a book by a contemporary black author. Who is the writer?

Comedy, Dance, and Fashion

7-33 By the 1960s and '70s, black comedians who dealt with political and social issues in a biting and satirical fashion began to emerge. Who was the best-known comedian of this school?

7-34 During the height of radio's popularity, a popular comedy show dealt with the black members of a fraternal lodge in Harlem. This show became a popular television series in the early days of television. What was the name of the show?

7-35 Alvin Ailey was a world-famous American choreographer. What was his dance theater (founded in 1958) known for?

7-36 Arthur Mitchell decided to "do in dance what Jackie Robinson did in baseball." What did he do?

7-37 During the 1960s colorful African-style shirts called Dashikis were often worn by black activists. What did the Dashiki symbolize?

7-38 What African-American hairstyle became popular in the 1960s, particularly among political activists?

7-39 From where does the African-American hairstyle known as dreadlocks come?

Intellectual Life

7-40 Since the 1960s, many American universities have created departments of Afro-American or black studies. To what was this a response?

7-41 By the 1990s, what controversies began to surround Afro-American studies programs at some universities?

7-42 In the last 20 years, an influential group of black scholars and intellectuals has broken away from the dominant "liberal" view of social policy. Who are some of the most important of these intellectuals, often labeled "conservatives"?

7-43 The growth in the number and influence of these black intellectuals is partly a reaction to the failure of the War on Poverty, launched in the 1960s to improve the plight of the bottom third of the black population. Explain the general view of this group.

7-44 These black intellectuals are critical of the traditional civil rights leadership and the role they have played in the past 30 years. What is the heart of their criticism?

Film and Television

7-45 In the early years of film and television, blacks generally were typecast as comical, clownish figures or as crooks and villains. What character type did Hattie McDaniel make famous in the movie *Gone with the Wind?*

7-46 In the 1950s, Hollywood began to break away from its demeaning, stereotypical portrayals of African Americans. What black actor was a trailblazer in showing that blacks could perform in serious dramatic roles without singing or dancing?

7-47 In the last 15 years, a number of independent black film producers and directors have made movies about the black experience from a black perspective. Who is the best known of these black film directors, and what are some of his most successful movies?

7-48 What black television personality starred in a situation comedy about a black upper-middle-class family? What was significant about this show?

7-49 African Americans have played a disproportionate role in all areas of contemporary American pop culture. What African-American woman has set the standard for popularity and celebrity as a talk show host?

African-American Artists

A lthough scholars have been slow to recognize the contributions of African Americans to the visual arts, African-American artistic traditions have been pervasive and influential over the
years—from the anonymous quilts of pre-Civil War times to the
post-World War II watercolors of Lois Mailou Jones. Some
notable figures in African-American art history: Robert Scott Dun-
canson (1817–72) was an important landscape artist and the first
African-American muralist. Henry O. Tanner (1859–1937) found
high acclaim for his painting in the more tolerant atmosphere of
turn-of-the-century France. Horace Pippin and Clementine
Hunter rank among 20th-century "primitivist" African-American
artists. During the Harlem Renaissance, Romare Bearden
emerged as a master of collage and Aaron Douglas infused new
life into African-American sculpture.

African-American artists have made innovations in both
traditional mediums like painting and sculpture, and more non-
traditional mediums. For example, quilting is an important area in
which African-American influence is strong and diverse. General
themes and techniques include improvisational strip quilting and
use of large shapes and strong colors, asymmetry, multiple
patterns in the same quilt, applique, diamond patterns, and script
(usually English, but occasionally in African languages in older
quilts). This is only a brief list; a wide variety of traditions and
methods of expression can be found within African-American
quilting.

◀ One of the most famous black abolitionists, Frederick Douglass was born a slave in 1817. After he escaped slavery in 1838, Douglass started speaking out against slavery and became a skilled orator. His autobiography, *Life and Times of Frederick Douglass,* was written to dispel any rumors that the well-spoken, literate Negro had not been a slave. During the Civil War, Douglass was an assistant to President Lincoln, and after the war he served in various political positions until his death in 1895.

CHAPTER

8

POLITICAL PARTICIPATION

The Abolition Movement and the Civil War

8-1 The Declaration of Independence refers to the proposition that all people are created equal and are endowed with "certain inalienable rights . . . life, liberty, and the pursuit of happiness." How did the founders of the United States reconcile this belief with the institution of slavery?

8-2 How did African Americans contribute to the War of Independence against Britain?

8-3 Why was the slave trade abolished by Congress in 1807?

8-4 In the South, some politicians began to support the end of the slave trade but for a different reason. What was their reason?

8-5 Most of the leading figures in the abolition movement were whites, but a sizable number of blacks rose to national prominence in the abolition cause. Name two of the most well known.

8-6 What novel written by a white woman helped win support for the abolition movement and was one of the most popular American books ever written?

8-7 In 1854, the Republican Party was formed. What was the main reason for its creation?

8-8 After the Civil War most black candidates elected to political office in the South were associated with the Republican Party. When did this association end?

8-9 The decision handed down by the U.S. Supreme Court in the Dred Scott case of 1857 was an important event leading up to the Civil War. What was this case about?

8-10 President Lincoln, although personally a great humanitarian, took a more ambiguous view of slavery as president. Describe his official position on this issue at the beginning of the Civil War.

8-11 As the Civil War dragged on, the Union army began to recruit black soldiers. How many African Americans fought on the side of the Union?

Reconstruction and Northern Politics

8-12 After the Civil War four amendments to the constitution had a huge influence on the position of blacks in American society. What were these amendments?

8-13 The 14th and 15th amendments were increasingly ignored in the South. What set of laws passed during the late 1800s made these amendments in practical terms meaningless in the South?

8-14 The last early African-American congressman from the South left Congress in 1901 at the height of the Jim Crow Laws. When did the next one get elected, and who was he?

8-15 The loyalty of African Americans to the Republican Party came to an end in the 1930s. What event caused blacks to switch party loyalties?

8-16 The association of the Republican Party with emancipation and black voting rights in the South had a huge impact on southern politics until the 1960s. What was this impact?

8-17 *Plessy v. Ferguson* in 1896 was the landmark Supreme Court case that legalized racial segregation. What was this case about?

8-18 The *Plessy v. Ferguson* decision had far-reaching effects on southern society. What were these effects?

8-19 Ida Wells was an African-American journalist and civil rights activist in the late 19th and early 20th centuries. With what issue was she most concerned?

8-20 Who was the first black senator to be elected to a full term?

8-21 Who was the next African American elected to the Senate?

8-22 Despite great efforts to woo blacks, the Communist Party in the United States never succeeded in attracting much support from African Americans, even during the Great Depression. What accounts for this failure?

8-23 Those few blacks who were drawn to communism or socialism were mostly intellectuals or public figures. Name some of these.

8-24 Paul Robeson was an outstanding singer, actor, and advocate of equality for African Americans. What did he do that tarnished his reputation?

The Civil Rights Era

8-25 In 1954, a famous court case called *Brown v. the Board of Education* went to the U.S. Supreme Court. What was this case about?

8-26 From 1955–65, blacks and whites were engaged in social and political activism known as the "The Movement." To what did this refer?

8-27 What two major black organizations were committed to winning civil rights?

8-28 Martin Luther King Jr. rose to prominence as a civil rights leader as a result of the Alabama bus boycott in 1955. What incident provoked this boycott?

8-29 What was unique about Dr. King's approach to winning civil rights for blacks?

8-30 In 1957 and 1963, federal troops and National Guardsmen had to accompany black students into public institutions. Why?

8-31 In the 1960s, the civil rights movement reached its peak. What event helped convince President Kennedy and his successor, President Johnson, that it was time to pass civil rights laws?

8-32 The climax of the civil rights movement occurred in 1963–65. What made the year 1963 a particularly striking anniversary for American blacks?

8-33 Resolving the issue of racial discrimination became paramount to American political leaders in the 1960s because of foreign policy as well as domestic peace. Explain why.

8-34 The civil rights movement in the 1950s and '60s was successful in achieving equal rights for blacks, although previous attempts had not been successful. What factors brought success this time?

8-35 The 1960s was an era of unprecedented economic prosperity for the United States. Why would this have an impact on white support for equal rights for blacks?

8-36 How were the conditions of the 1960s different from those of the 1860s Reconstruction years in determining the attitudes of southern whites toward black demands for equality?

8-37 In 1966, after the Voting Rights Act was passed, six members of Congress were black. In 1992, there were 40 black congressmen. What caused such a dramatic increase in black representation in 25 years?

8-38 The Black Power wing of the civil rights movement got a boost from the assassination of Martin Luther King Jr. Why was this so?

8-39 What effect did the Black Power and Black Panther movements have on the inner-city youth of the 1960s and '70s?

8-40 Bayard Rustin was one of the leading figures in the civil rights movement of the 1950s and '60s. What distinguished him from some of his colleagues?

The Post-Civil Rights Era

8-41 What happened to the opponents of civil rights in the South after federal laws and Supreme Court decisions went into effect in the 1960s?

8-42 Jesse Jackson founded the Rainbow Coalition in the 1980s. What was this political organization meant to accomplish?

8-43 What happened to the Rainbow Coalition?

8-44 Gary Frank and J. C. Watts, two black congressmen elected in the 1990s, represent a new breed of black politician. What makes them different from their predecessors?

8-45 The increasing racial and ethnic diversity of the American population will have an impact on black political power and representation in the future. Explain why this is true.

8-46 Which African head of state toured the United States in the early 1990s and was given a hero's welcome by all Americans, but especially by African Americans?

8-47 Have African Americans shown much interest in the affairs of African nations?

Speaking Out Against Slavery

In the fight for abolition at the beginning of the 19th century, slave narratives became a popular and successful means of spreading the message against slavery. These were often first-person accounts of the narrator's life as a slave and stories about the general conditions of slavery. Slave narratives ranged from sentimental to horrifying in tone in their attempts to illustrate the experience of the cruelty of slavery. *Narrative of the Life of Frederick Douglass, An American Slave* was perhaps the most well-known and most influential of these books.

Because escape from slavery was illegal, and an ex-slave could have been returned to slavery, many writers of slave narratives had to write anonymously or under pseudonyms. The writers were often accused of making up their stories because they wrote under these false names. One such example was a writer named "Linda Brent." Until the late 1980s, her slave narrative, *Incidents in the Life of a Slave Girl,* was considered by many to be fake, written by a white abolitionist, because historical documents showed no trace of a real person named Linda Brent. But by tracing the story of her life, historians have found that Linda Brent did exist. Her real name was Harriet Jacobs, and her story, in which she spent seven years hidden in a crawlspace to escape, still proves a powerful testament to the horrors of slavery.

◀ In 1988, Dr. Mae C. Jemison became the fifth black astronaut, and the first female African-American astronaut, in the history of the National Aeronautics and Space Administration (NASA). Before her selection as an astronaut by NASA, Jemison graduated from Stanford University and the Cornell University School of Medicine, and worked in the Peace Corps as a medical officer.

CHAPTER 9

IMPORTANT PERSONALITIES and PEOPLE OF ACCOMPLISHMENT

Intellectual and Cultural Figures

9-1 Which son of slaves was the first black mathematician, astronomer, inventor, and almanac publisher in America?

9-2 George Washington Carver was one of the first black scientists in America. For what is he best known?

9-3 Which African American worked with Thomas Edison and invented a method for producing carbon filaments for electric lightbulbs?

9-4 Elijah McCoy was a 19th-century black inventor. What type of mechanical inventions is he credited with, and what else is he known for?

9-5 Mary MacLeod Bethune, the daughter of sharecroppers from South Carolina, is known for what accomplishment?

9-6 Marian Anderson was an accomplished black singer of the 1930s. What is she most known for today?

9-7 What black writer originally from the British West Indies recently won a Nobel Prize for literature?

Elected and Appointed Public Figures

9-8 The first Nobel Peace Prize won by an African American was awarded to Ralph Bunche in 1950. For what accomplishment was he given the prize?

9-9 What leader of the NAACP during the civil rights struggles of the 1950s was appointed the first black justice on the Supreme Court?

9-10 Adam Clayton Powell was the most influential black congressman for several decades (1950s and 1960s). What district did he represent?

9-11 Thomas Bradley was elected mayor of Los Angeles in 1973 at a time when many American cities elected their first black mayors. What was unusual about his election?

9-12 Who was the first black mayor of New York City?

9-13 Who was the second black person to be appointed to the Supreme Court?

Sports

9-14 Who was the first African American to participate in Major League Baseball, paving the way for the integration of the sport?

9-15 Which black boxer was world champion for a record 12 years?

9-16 Which black boxer in the 1960s captured the media spotlight with his winning record, outgoing personality, and clever quips?

9-17 Jesse Owens was a great track star who won four gold medals at the Berlin Olympics in 1936. What memorable incident at these Olympics is associated with Jesse Owens?

9-18 What black woman won three gold medals in the 1960 Olympics, establishing a record for Olympic achievement by a woman?

9-19 For several decades the majority of players in the National Basketball Association have been black. Approximately what percentage of players are African American today?

9-20 What major championships was Arthur Ashe the first African-American man to win?

9-21 What African-American woman won both Wimbledon and the U.S. Open in two consecutive years?

9-22 Which black baseball player broke Babe Ruth's record for the number of home runs hit in a career?

Military Service

9-23 Who was the first black brigadier general in the U.S. Army?

9-24 Who was the first African American to be appointed chairman of the Joint Chiefs of Staff of the Armed Forces?

CHAPTER

10 Answers

◄ President Lyndon B. Johnson
signs the National Voting Rights
Act in 1965 as a group of supporters, including the Rev. Martin
Luther King Jr., looks on.

ANSWERS
CHAPTER

1 ORIGINS

Life in Early Africa

1-1 The ancestors of most African Americans came from the western coast of Africa. Specifically, they came from the present-day countries of Ghana, Mali, Benin, Nigeria, and Angola.

1-2 Most, if not all, Africans were animists. They believed that all earthly objects contain good and evil spirits that have to be satisfied through worship and sacrifices.

1-3 Africans believed that the spirits of ancestors continued to take an interest in the family after their death.

1-4 They lived among members of their extended family, mostly in farming villages or temporary encampments. They had noble classes and royalty as well as the workers and farmers who made up most of the population.

1-5 The clan's patriarch, or male leader, was seen as a go-between with ancestral spirits.

1-6 An African clan unit was generally composed of all the descendants of a common ancestor—whether a man or a woman. Some African social groups were patriarchal (headed by men), and some were matriarchal (headed by women).

1-7 Repeated incursions and attacks by Arab nomadic tribes from across the Sahara desert forced African clans to create larger and more formal political entities for their own self-defense.

1-8 Gold.

1-9 The Kingdom of Mali.

1-10 The Empire of Songhai.

1-11 African kings wanted to control the increasing number of trade routes being established in West Africa between the 11th and 15th centuries. The larger number of trade routes a king controlled, the more power he had and the more tributes he received from his subjects.

1-12 African empires extended over hundreds of miles in every direction and were probably as large as most of Western Europe.

Africa During the Period of Muslim and European Contacts

1-13 From the 11th century onward, the ruling class and the merchant class among the Africans began to convert to Islam. The common people remained faithful to local African religions and were untouched by Islam until many centuries later.

1-14 Some Africans converted under pressure because of Islamic conquest. Other Africans converted because there were economic advantages to being a Muslim when dealing with Arab traders and merchants. Some Africans were attracted by the egalitarian nature of Islam and its nonracial approach to religious education and community life.

▲ Muslims in Zaire pray to mark the Feast of Sacrifice, which commemorates the prophet Abraham's willingness to offer his son as a sacrifice to God. Many Africans and African Americans follow Islam, which requires prayers, or *salat*, five times a day. The prayer ritual—standing, kneeling, and touching the ground with the forehead—can be performed anywhere as long as the worshipper faces Islam's holy city, Mecca.

1-15   When African clans or tribes engaged in warfare, the victorious tribe would often use captured members of the losing tribe as slaves. The slaves functioned as unpaid servants, and their children were often freed. Captured slaves were also used as a form of barter in trading with other African tribes.

1-16   Arab Muslim invasions in the 7th to 11th centuries changed slavery from a local institution to an international one. Muslims used their slaves mainly as house servants or in the harem of a tribal chief or other notable. They did not use slaves to increase economic production. They chiefly took women and children as slaves.

1-17 Arab Muslims justified their involvement in slavery because they believed the injunction against slavery applied only to Muslims. Thus, "infidels" (people who were not Muslims) could be enslaved. Africans who were taken as slaves by the Arab traders were considered infidels because they were followers of African religions.

1-18 Europeans saw the slave trade as a source for human labor in the New World. This labor force became the basis for an entire economic system. Europeans primarily took men as slaves.

1-19 Some Europeans rationalized that slavery was necessary to bring about the conversion of heathen populations. Others rationalized slavery by explaining that Africans were an inferior race.

1-20 Portugal started its involvement in the slave trade in the late 15th century.

1-21 Africans traded gold and slaves to the Portuguese.

1-22 European merchants established fortresses on the coast of Africa and traded goods to African kings in exchange for slaves. Europeans rarely ventured inland in Africa. They feared disease and lacked a common language with most Africans.

1-23 The British were the dominant power in the transatlantic slave trade from 1650 to 1807, when they abolished it altogether. The Dutch and French were also involved in this commerce, but to a lesser extent.

▲ In the 19th century, European powers like Great Britain, France, and Portugal carved out colonies in Africa, often using force to conquer the native tribes that ruled each region. This is the artillery train of an invading British army in the mountains of Ethiopia around 1868.

1-24 The British and Portuguese traded manufactured goods to the African chiefs who sold them slaves. The Europeans then sold the slaves to plantation owners in the New World in exchange for sugar, tobacco, and cotton.

1-25 Slavery was outlawed in Britain and throughout the British Empire largely for humanitarian reasons. Most of the religious and civil leaders in Britain by the 19th century were opposed to the slave trade.

1-26 The Muslim-controlled slave trade continued into the second half of the 20th century.

1-27 It is estimated that between 10 million and 12 million slaves were involved in the transatlantic slave trade. About 15 million slaves are estimated to have been involved in the slave trade to the Middle East.

The West Indies

1-28 The islands that make up the West Indies were major centers for the production of sugar. Growing sugarcane takes a lot of manual labor. Slaves were used as a source of cheap labor.

1-29 Haiti was originally a French colony with an economy based on slave labor. In 1804, a slave revolt drove out the French and resulted in the permanent establishment of a new nation.

1-30 During the fight for independence, Toussaint L'Ouverture abolished slavery in Haiti in 1801.

2 ARRIVAL IN AMERICA

The Slave Trade and the South

2-1 Of the 10 million to 12 million slaves who were brought across the Atlantic, only about 400,000 actually came to America (about 5 percent of the total). The rest went to South America and the Caribbean Islands.

2-2 Slavery had already existed in the New World when the first Europeans arrived in the 15th and 16th centuries. The Mayas and Aztecs owned slaves—usually either prisoners of war or criminals. The Spanish and Portugese had used African slaves on their plantations on the Iberian peninsula, and they brought Africans with them when they came to the Americas. They also attempted to enslave the Native Americans; however, the population of this group was so small, and its mortality rate so high, that African slaves had to be imported to the New World to meet increased demand for sugar, cotton, and tobacco production, as well as mining.

When colonists from Great Britain settled in the southern region of North America in the 17th century, the demand for cheap labor led to the importation of poor workers from Europe. These people, looking for a new life in the New World, promised to work as servants for a period of years in exchange for their passage across the Atlantic Ocean and the cost of clothing, housing, and feeding them. The number of indentured servants began to drop by the late 17th century, as many of them earned their freedom.

2-3 Exact statistics are not known, but it is estimated that 20 to 30 percent of the slaves shipped from Africa died before reaching the New World.

2-4 Many died of disease on the journey across the ocean (the "middle passage"). Others committed suicide or were disabled by disease or captivity.

2-5 Chattel slavery was the type of slavery reserved for blacks in colonial America. It was instituted at the end of the 17th century. Under this system, black people were treated as pieces of property by their owners, with no rights. The children of chattel slaves were also considered the property of their parent's owners.

▼ With the end of the Civil War in 1865, emancipated African Americans migrated to major cities in order to start new lives. Cities like Baltimore witnessed the arrival of freedmen and their families on a daily basis.

2-6 More than 90 percent of African slaves were settled in the South. Less than 10 percent went to the Northeast.

2-7 Fewer slaves were used in the North for two reasons: a) The northern economy was based on small family farms and craftsmanship and therefore had no use for large numbers of unskilled laborers. The South, in contrast, had an economy based on plantations that produced a few labor-intensive crops—sugar, tobacco, and cotton. b) Many northerners opposed slavery on religious and moral grounds.

2-8 The slave trade was abolished by Congress in 1807. Illegal smuggling of slaves continued for a number of decades, but British antislavery patrols on the high seas made these operations increasingly difficult.

2-9 Relatively few Africans were brought as slaves to the United States after the English abolished the trade in 1808. The number of slaves continued to grow primarily through childbirth. The birth rate among African-American slaves was quite high.

Black Migration to the North and West

2-10 Buffalo soldiers was a nickname given to the Ninth and Tenth U.S. cavalries, two units of black soldiers formed after the Civil War that served in the frontier territory in the West. They fought along with other army units against Native Americans and helped establish military outposts in the West. The term later became a nickname for any member of an all-black military unit.

2-11 From 1910 to 1970, a huge wave of blacks moved from the rural South to the urban areas of the North and South. This movement completely changed the social characteristics and geographic distribution of African Americans.

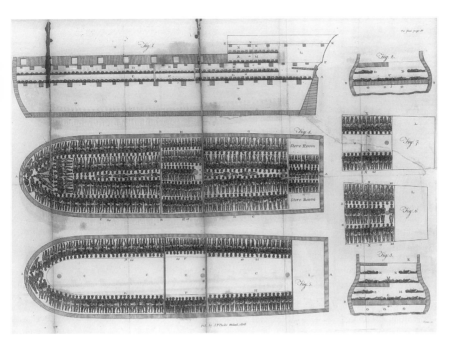

▲ A drawing of a slave ship shows the cramped living spaces that Africans had to endure in the two to three month journey to America. "Loose pack" ships allotted a space measuring approximately six feet long and one foot wide to each captive. "Tight pack" ships did not even afford the slaves enough room to lie on their backs. On the average slave ship, between 20 and 30 percent of the captives died, largely due to lack of food, poor ventilation, and the spread of disease.

2-12 Before the 20th century, African Americans lived primarily in small towns or rural areas of the South. As a result of moving north, a large number of African Americans settled in the industrial cities of the Northeast and Midwest.

2-13 Until 1940, the population of the North was only four percent black. Most northern cities had one sizable black neighborhood and a stable black middle class dispersed in other neighborhoods as well. As large numbers of southern blacks began to settle in neighborhoods formerly occupied by white natives and immigrants, whites began to move to the suburbs. The black middle class joined the exodus to the suburbs as well. Many of the remaining black neighborhoods in inner cities began suffering from high concentrations of poverty and social problems.

2-14 In many cases, hostility and violence occurred as African Americans began to move into the neighborhoods populated by European immigrants, especially in northern cities. These immigrants had cultural backgrounds that were very different from the culture of the southern blacks who were migrating north; racial tensions occasionally flared into riots. In the "red summer" of 1919, dozens of race riots occurred in cities throughout the country. In the South, the Ku Klux Klan, an organization created after the Civil War to terrorize southern blacks, experienced a resurgence in membership and initiated a wave of lynchings in the 1920s and '30s.

2-15 Harlem is a neighborhood in upper Manhattan that has been the largest and most well-known black urban community in the country from the 1920s until today. In the 1920s, it was known for its lively entertainment and as a center of black intellectual and cultural life. Later it fell into decay. There is an attempt to revive the neighborhood today because of its symbolism as the center of African-American life.

2-16 For the first time in the 20th century more blacks were moving from North to South than the other way around.

2-17 The "New South" no longer has legalized discrimination and segregation. Much of this region is also enjoying an economic boom, and industry is relocating from northern cities.

2-18 The Fair Housing Act barred racial discrimination in the sale or rental of housing.

2-19 Although inner cities are disproportionately black and poor, there has been a large movement of upwardly mobile blacks out of the cities into the suburbs since 1970. (From 1970 to 1990, six million blacks moved from cities to suburbs).

2-20 Middle- and working-class blacks are moving to the suburbs for the same reasons that second- and third-generation European Americans did: better housing, less crowding, good public schools, and less crime.

Immigration from the West Indies and Africa

2-21 In 1965 the United States Congress changed the immigration laws. Since then there has been a large influx of black immigrants from Haiti, the Guianas, Jamaica, and other small islands. Most immigrants from the Dominican Republic are considered racially black, but they are culturally Hispanic.

2-22 Many middle-class Haitians who opposed the repressive policies of the Duvalier regime fled the island during those years.

2-23 Greater New York.

2-24 Like most immigrants, Haitians prefer living with people from their own background. They speak either French or Creole and are mostly Catholic, unlike African Americans, who speak English and are mostly Protestant.

2-25 British West Indians of the early 20th century were almost universally literate, and most were skilled or white-collar workers.

2-26 Most of these Africans have immigrated to the United States because of civil wars in their homelands (Ethiopia, Eritrea, Somalia) or for economic reasons.

3 ECONOMIC LIFE

▲ Displaying the same courage that they had shown during the Civil War nearly a century before, the African-American soldiers of World War II fought proudly for their country. Here, Sergeant Franklin Williams leads his army unit, the 41st Engineers, in a parade-field march at Fort Bragg, North Carolina, in 1942.

The Plantation System

3-1 North and South America and the Caribbean were sparsely populated and rich in land and water resources. They were perfectly suited to large scale, labor-intensive agriculture. Slaves would be easy to control because they would be far from the places they had come from and socially isolated. They also cost land owners much less money than would hired workers.

3-2 In 1793, Eli Whitney invented the cotton gin. This, combined with the Industrial Revolution beginning in Britain, made the increased cultivation of cotton very profitable for southern plantations. From the 1790s until the Civil War, the slave population grew mostly in the cotton-growing states of the deep South where the export of this crop was the basis of economic life.

3-3 Cotton was exported to the northern states and to England.

3-4 About 75 percent of slaves were involved in cotton production.

3-5 Slave masters prohibited their slaves from learning to read because they were afraid their slaves might read about life in the North or get "radical" ideas about freedom and equality and begin to plot rebellions.

The Post-Slavery South

3-6 Freed slaves had no property, and very few of them had job skills except as farmers. Thus, most southern blacks became *sharecroppers,* or tenant farmers, who often lived in debt to the landowners—not much better off than when they were slaves.

3-7 Crop failures, mechanization of agriculture, the boll weevil, and soil depletion pushed black workers out of agricultural labor. In addition, many blacks thought that the North would be a better place to live because of its greater racial tolerance. Also, the North was undergoing an industrial revolution and there was a constant demand for unskilled labor.

3-8   The insurance industry and in particular the North Carolina Mutual Life Insurance Company.

3-9   White-run insurance companies in the South in the late 1800s refused to insure blacks because they considered them high-risk clients. This left the market open to black entrepreneurs. They were able to insure African Americans with no competition well into the 20th century.

Urban Life

3-10   African Americans were excluded from many labor unions that offered opportunities for upward mobility. They also had difficulty becoming apprentices to northern craftsmen because of racist attitudes and because immigrant craftsmen tended to give opportunities to members of their own ethnic group first.

3-11   The white union leadership said it believed in the solidarity of the working class but the white laborers themselves didn't want blacks in the union—partly because of fear that they would lose jobs and partly due to racial animosity.

3-12   The AFL was afraid of disrupting and weakening the newly born labor movement, and it recognized the depth of racial hostility toward blacks harbored by many of the union's members.

3-13   The Congress of Industrial Organizations (CIO) led the way under the leadership of John L. Lewis. The CIO, which included the International Ladies Garment Work-

▲ A. Philip Randolph (1889-1979) was a proponent of civil rights. Randolph was cofounder of the radical journal *Messenger,* was president of the National Negro Congress, and instigated a number of protests against racial discrimination, including the famous March for Jobs and Freedom rally of 1963. In 1964, Randolph was presented with the Presidential Medal of Freedom for his tireless efforts in the fight for equality.

ers Union (ILGWU)—always the most racially inclusive of all the unions—later merged with the AFL.

3-14 He insisted in the 1940s that black workers be fully integrated into the union and be given the same conditions and benefits as white workers.

3-15 A. Philip Randolph.

3-16 Having African Americans such as Randolph and Willard Townsend in leading positions in the union symbolized the important role that blacks played in the American working class. Although they made up only 11 percent of the American population in the 1950s, blacks were a much larger percentage of the blue-collar labor force.

3-17 Several prominent black leaders began to organize a march on Washington to pressure the federal government to guarantee equal employment opportunity in the defense industry. President Roosevelt agreed to issue an executive order in 1941 requiring an end to racial discrimination for federal jobs if the organizers would agree to call off the march. The executive order was the first attempt by the federal government to guarantee blacks equal access to jobs in government and industry. It included ways to enforce the order. The result of this executive order was an immediate rise in the number of blacks in both government and industry.

3-18 Employment in defense-related industries helped to give black workers entrance into the skilled blue-collar workforce. In 1940 only approximately 30 percent of black workers had jobs requiring skill. By 1945, 50 percent of black workers were in skilled positions. This led to a huge expansion of the black middle class.

3-19 Twenty percent.

3-20 Affirmative action was designed as a program to increase admission rates of African Americans at colleges and universities and to increase African American employment. Institutions or corporations that had previously discriminated against qualified blacks or had not made strong efforts to recruit them were required by law to change their policies.

3-21 Most white and many Asian Americans now oppose these policies on the grounds that American society has changed substantially in the last 30 years. They think that qualified blacks (and Hispanics) no longer need policies that have gradually come to be seen as forms of preferential treatment. African Americans are divided on this issue, although most blacks still support some form of affirmative action.

3-22 Berry Gordy was the entrepreneur who founded the legendary Motown recording company and showed that African American recording stars could appeal to a universal audience.

3-23 Carmichael was referring to the reservoir of potential black political power just created by the Voting Rights Act of 1965. He exhorted blacks to assert themselves in order to control their own destinies, rather than allowing the broader society to dictate their fate to them.

3-24 *Fortune*'s article dealt with the rise to prominence of a successful class of black entrepreneurs and business executives since the 1960s. From 1987 to 1992, the number of black-owned businesses rose from 420,000 to 620,000.

3-25 In 1996 the top 100 black-owned businesses had revenues of $14 billion.

3-26 This group of African Americans faces many social problems, such as single-parent families, poor job opportunities in the inner cities, drug abuse, and poor education. All of these problems contribute to the continuation of poverty.

3-27 Queens has the largest concentration of middle-class blacks anywhere in the United States. The average household income of blacks in Queens is higher than that of whites in the same area.

3-28 The military is one of the few institutions in this society where career success is almost entirely based on performance and merit. Family connections, previous experience, and wealth play no role here, which means people from underprivileged backgrounds are not at a professional disadvantage.

3-29 More black leaders promote private enterprise and middle-class culture as keys to urban renewal rather than relying on welfare programs, as was emphasized in the 1960s.

3-30 In 1999, the Upper Manhattan Empowerment Zone managed by Deborah Wright is planning to open a $56-million mall called Harlem USA. In Detroit, Mayor Dennis Archer has convinced Chrysler to build a $900-million plant in the city—the first new automobile plant built there in many years. And in Cleveland, Mayor Michael White has helped revitalize what was once considered a decaying rust-belt city into one of the most livable and thriving urban areas in the country.

4 RELIGIOUS LIFE

The Old South and Christianity

4-1 By the late 18th century, Christianity began to spread among the slaves. These conversions were mainly among slaves born into captivity and not among those who had been raised in Africa.

4-2 Some plantation owners restricted the subjects of sermons so slaves wouldn't be encouraged to look forward to freedom from slavery, one of the themes in the Bible. In addition, the plantation owners would supply the white preachers. In spite of these efforts, slaves learned stories about the ancient Hebrews being freed from slavery and about Jesus dying to free people from the power of sin.

4-3 *Nobody knows the trouble I've seen.*
Nobody knows but Jesus.
Nobody knows the trouble I've seen.
Glory Hallelujah!
During the years of slavery, black religious life was limited by the conditions of plantation life. One of the few outlets for religious expression was the spiritual. These spirituals typically refer to the harshness of slavery and the redeeming power of God.

4-4 Some of the best loved spirituals are those that refer to the ancient Israelites held captive by the Pharaoh, as in "Go Down, Moses," or other stories from the Old Testament, such as the story of Elijah and heaven's chariot in "Swing

▲ Churchgoers at Father Divine in Harlem sing an inspirational hymn. Religion plays a large part in the lives of many black families, many of whom are practicing Christians. Music often plays a significant part in African-American church services, and gospel music is a popular way of expressing prayer through song.

Low, Sweet Chariot" or Joshua's victory at Jericho in "Joshua Fit the Battle of Jericho."

4-5 The slavery of the ancient Hebrews and their subsequent redemption was one theme that gave American slaves hope. They also took inspiration from the image of going to the Promised Land and building a new Zion in America.

The Growth of Black Churches

4-6 Blacks were not treated as religious equals in Protestant churches, and they felt that equality of worship could only be achieved in a separate church. In addition, the black style of worship was distinctly different from that used in white churches. The black church was known for the oratorical style of its preachers, the expressiveness and responsive participation of its congregations, and its unique types of music.

4-7 Chanted sermons are characterized by spontaneity, improvisation, and establishing a rapport with the congregation.

4-8 Black churches sponsored benevolent societies, charities, and educational instruction in places where there were no public schools for black children.

4-9 The Ebenezer Baptist Church is the church where Martin Luther King Jr. preached his first and last sermons. His father and grandfather were also pastors at this church, which was at the center of black civil rights activities in the South during the entire 20th century.

4-10 Black churches rapidly became the training ground of an independent and educated black leadership after the Civil War and through the 20th century. Most of the leaders of the civil rights movement in the 1950s and '60s were ministers of black churches.

Recent Trends

4-11 Catholicism, Judaism, and Islam.

4-12 The number of black Catholics rose in the last 50 years to roughly four percent of the black population (excluding the Haitian population). Black Muslims now make up three to five percent of the population. There are a number of black Jewish congregations and individual blacks who have converted into the Jewish community as well.

4-13 Voodoo, Santeria, and Rastafarianism.

4-14 Rastafarianism is a religion that began in Jamaica in the 1930s. It was related to Marcus Garvey's political and social movement (Garvey was Jamaican). It emphasizes the African roots of blacks and considers Ethiopia to be the black homeland.

4-15 Rastafarianism was embraced by a large segment of the poor black population of Jamaica, and certain elements of it have been brought to America by Jamaican immigrants and by fans of reggae music (another Jamaican import).

4-16 Many blacks who live in urban areas that are beset by social breakdown and disorder are attracted to religious movements that emphasize discipline, respect for authority, and community life.

4-17 A sizable minority of the students who attend Catholic schools in northern cities are black.

4-18 Black parents in inner cities like the discipline, religious values, and high academic standards of the Catholic schools. They frequently find these qualities missing in the public schools.

4-19 Wallace Fard established the Lost-Found Nation of Islam. He was succeeded by Elijah Muhammad, who revived the almost-defunct movement and shaped the Nation of Islam into its modern form.

4-20 Originally Elijah Muhammad saw his movement as a return to the original "African" religion of many blacks, which he saw as Islam. However, his version of Islam— drawn from the teachings of Wallace Fard—was based on the idea that blacks should segregate themselves from whites and disassociate themselves from as much of "white" culture as they could. By the time he died in 1975, he had moderated this view.

4-21 Historians calculate that roughly 20 percent of the original African slaves were Muslims.

4-22 Malcolm X made a pilgrimage to Mecca. There he came into contact with Muslims of all races who had mutually respectful relationships. He realized that the Muslim faith does not distinguish among people on the basis of race. He returned to America believing that people of different races can coexist peacefully.

5 SOCIAL LIFE AND INSTITUTIONS

Plantation Life and Slavery

5-1 Slavery disrupted black family life. Many slave owners did not allow their slaves to marry and often broke up families by selling the husband or wife to someone else. Nevertheless, the slaves on plantations made a great effort to sustain family life.

5-2 Nat Turner was a slave who led a bloody uprising in 1831 in Virginia. Turner and his band of male slaves killed 61 white men, women, and children, most of whom lived on small farms. Seeking revenge, white men killed an unknown number of black people who had no connection to the revolt. These black people were not given trials and were killed in cold blood—some by decapitation. Nat Turner himself was captured, tried, and executed.

5-3 Generally the slaves who worked in the fields had the lowest status. The work supervisors had higher status, and the slaves who worked in the household service of the master had the highest status.

5-4 The Quakers, who were leaders in the antislavery movement, were very active and numerous in Pennsylvania.

5-5 The Colonization Society sought to resettle American blacks in Africa, specifically in a country called Liberia.

5-6 Some slaveowners supported colonization of free blacks to better preserve the institution of slavery. They feared the presence of free blacks would incite slaves to rebel. Some whites thought that blacks would be better off going back to Africa. Some thought that returning blacks to Africa would bring the benefits of Christianity and Western civilization to Africa.

5-7 Very few African Americans wanted to return to Africa. The ones who favored colonization preferred to establish a colony somewhere within the territory of the United States, such as in the Missouri River Valley.

5-8 The Underground Railroad was the name given to the system through which antislavery activists secretly helped slaves escape from the South to freedom in the North or Canada before the Civil War. Whites, free blacks, and Native Americans participated in this effort.

5-9 The movement initially had the character of a religious crusade because many of its supporters were active in churches and the rationale for abolition came from Christian beliefs. The movement was also part of a broader spirit of reform sweeping Europe and the northern United States in the mid-1800s.

5-10 The prominent whites were New York businessmen Arthur and Lewis Tappan, poet John Greenleaf Whittier, writer Harriet Beecher Stowe, militant John Brown, and editor William Lloyd Garrison. The prominent blacks were orator and editor Frederick Douglass, Underground Railroad conductor Harriet Tubman, and writer William Wells Brown, among many others.

5-11 Douglass was an important figure not only because of his talent, but also as a symbol of a freed black man. He was a runaway slave who was self-educated. He became an impressive orator and wrote several autobiographical

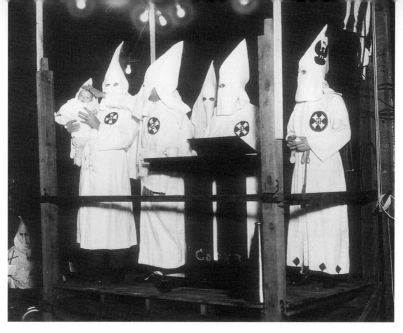

▲ Dedication of an infant to the Ku Klux Klan. Founded in 1866 by former Confederate soldiers, the Klan soon became known for its violence against African Americans. Their white-hooded robes and symbol—a burning cross—were common sights, especially in the South, until the 1930s when the Klan lost most of its power.

accounts of his life both as a slave and as a free man. His life story was proof that a freed slave could take responsibility for himself and become a leader of other people.

5-12 The Emancipation Proclamation took effect on January 1, 1863.

The South After the Civil War

5-13 Washington felt that in order to make themselves economically viable in a modern economy, blacks should acquire technical skills, vocational education, and attitudes of self-reliance and entrepreneurialism. He became head of the Tuskegee Institute in 1881. The institute's mission was to achieve those objectives.

5-14 Spelman College was established in Atlanta in 1882.

5-15 One hundred colleges.

5-16 The Ku Klux Klan underwent a revival in the 1920s partly as a reaction to the huge influx of immigrants during the previous 40 years. The Klan spread beyond the South and became a national movement that opposed not only blacks, but also Jews, Catholics, and Asians.

City Life

5-17 Bishop Henry McNeal Turner launched his "Back to Africa" scheme in the 1890s. He saw Liberia as a home for black Americans, but the idea collapsed quickly. Marcus Garvey used his United Negro Improvement Association as the basis for his movement in the 1920s. He also encouraged black Americans to settle in Liberia. This scheme failed as well.

5-18 The NAACP was founded in 1909; the National Urban League in 1910; and the Commission on Interracial Cooperation in 1919.

5-19 W. E. B. DuBois made this statement in the early years of the 20th century. He believed educated black people would lift the entire race by setting an example and guiding the African-American community.

5-20 Many blacks of the lower social and economic levels didn't think that organizations like the NAACP were interested in their problems. They felt that these groups functioned mainly as vehicles for the advancement of the black middle class.

5-21 Garvey staged impressive public events in major cities. He appealed to black pride and racial solidarity and urged blacks to be proud of their African roots. His movement encouraged and aided the establishment of black businesses. He exhorted American blacks to return to Africa and build it into a glorious empire.

5-22 Even though his movement failed to achieve its purpose and Garvey was later jailed for mail fraud and deported, the movement was significant for two reasons:

1) It was the first mass movement of African Americans organized from within the black community.

2) It showed that African Americans wanted to stay in America and improve their lot rather than go back to Africa. The support Garvey received was more a protest against how African Americans were being treated after World War I than an expression of serious interest in Garvey's schemes.

5-23 The exclusion of black men from many types of unionized jobs blocked their upward mobility. Black men became demoralized and lost authority in their families. The difficulty of transplanting black churches to rapidly-growing poor urban neighborhoods also deprived younger generations of the main source of moral education that had existed in the black community in the South.

Post-World War II America

5-24 After the war, popular reaction to the horror of the Nazi genocide of the Jews made many Americans reconsider their treatment of blacks, and discriminatory policies against other minorities. The valorous participation of blacks in the U.S. war effort (mostly in all-black units) had an impact on public opinion as well.

5-25 Black soldiers performed bravely and effectively in World War II, and toward the end of the war they fought in several integrated units with successful results. This plus the general growth in tolerance and the push after the war toward greater inclusion of minority groups in American society led to the change in policy.

5-26 Eldridge Cleaver moved to Algeria for many years and then returned to America. He later became a born-again Chris-

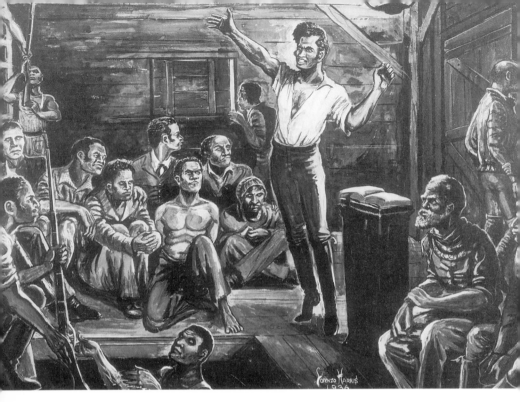

▲ Before the abolition of slavery, there were at least 30 uprisings staged by slaves against their masters. In the early 1830s Nat Turner, a slave, led one of the bloodiest revolts. Over 50 people were killed by 70 rebellious slaves before the uprising was quashed. Unfortunately, rather than improving conditions, the revolt led to greater restrictions on slaves.

tian and evangelist. Stokely Carmichael moved to Africa and settled permanently in Guinea, where he became involved in African politics. He changed his name to Kwame Ture. Neither man attracted many imitators.

5-27 They were boldly defiant of white authority at a time when that attitude was in vogue among radical younger community leaders. They promised a redistribution of wealth from the rich to the poor and imitated some of the slogans and poses of Third World liberation movements popular at the time.

5-28 The Panthers advocated the use of violence against the police in the name of self-defense. The founder of the party, Huey Newton, was put in jail for shooting a policeman. Other members were arrested on various charges, and internal feuds finally destroyed what was left of the organization by the 1970s.

5-29 Marcus Garvey supported these ideas but with a different long-term goal. He suggested that blacks should return to Africa and establish their own civilization. Black Muslim leaders Elijah Muhammad, Malcolm X, and later Louis Farrakhan have also advocated views similar to Washington's. Unlike Washington, however, the Black Muslims adopted an antagonistic attitude toward whites, and for the most part they have not supported reconciliation between the races. Today a group of black conservatives is seeking a return to the original meaning of Booker T. Washington's views. This group supports a revival of black community life without an emphasis on integration but in a spirit of cooperation with whites and other races.

5-30 Farrakhan is similarly charismatic and dramatic. Like Garvey, he believes that whites and blacks can't coexist with a relationship based on equality. Like Garvey, he argues that blacks should be self-reliant and proud of their race. However, Farrakhan does not support a return of American blacks to Africa.

5-31 Most blacks in the 1920s supported Garvey as a way of expressing their discontent and as a comment on the failures of the existing black leadership to win civil rights. Most of the blacks who support Farrakhan do so also as a statement of their discontent and not as an endorsement of his racial hatred and anti-Semitism.

5-32 It was founded to strengthen ties between black Americans and other scattered African populations and to serve as a lobby to promote economic and political ties between America and countries with black populations.

6 GROUP CHARACTERISTICS

ANSWERS
CHAPTER

Demographic Data

6-1 In 1860, about four million blacks lived in slavery.

6-2 Half a million free blacks, over 10 percent of the black population, lived in America in 1860. Half the free blacks lived in the South.

6-3 Some were granted their freedom by their masters, and some bought their freedom through wage labor. The 250,000 free blacks in the North were mostly runaway slaves or slaves who had been freed by their masters, or their descendants.

6-4 Mississippi, Louisiana, and South Carolina.

6-5 About 50 percent.

6-6 Over 30 million.

6-7 Over 50 percent.

6-8 A large increase in the number of black students attending other American colleges began in the 1960s. By 1984, only 27 percent of black students were enrolled in historically black colleges.

6-9 Black Americans who descended from freed slaves (85 to 90 percent); West Indian immigrants and their descen-

▲ Colin Powell made history when President George Bush appointed him the chairman of the Joint Chiefs of Staff, the United States' top military post, in 1989. Powell
was not only the first African-American to receive the honor, he was the youngest
man as well.

dants (about 10 percent); recent African immigrants and
their children (1 percent); and people of mixed race
background (partly black and partly another race, primarily white) who do not choose to identify themselves
as black (1 percent).

6-10 Since immigration laws were changed in 1965, America
has absorbed a large influx of people from Asia, Latin
America, and the Middle East, most of whom are not
considered white (although many of them have some
European ancestry). People of European descent officially made up 89 percent of the U.S. population in 1950
and 75 percent in 1990.

Class and Social Divisions

6-11 One view, initially articulated by W. E. B. DuBois, was that support should go to the "Talented Tenth," the top 10 percent of the black population who would be its elite leadership. This philosophy has guided the NAACP in fighting against legal and social barriers for blacks since its founding. The other view, supported initially by Booker T. Washington, was that effort should be invested in the other 90 percent who needed to acquire basic literacy, vocational and entrepreneurial skills, and good citizenship attitudes to make them successful as free citizens.

6-12 The black leadership after the Civil War was dominated by free blacks and their descendants probably because of their greater literacy and intergenerational experience in living in an open, competitive society.

6-13 He is referring to the polarization of the black population. Roughly one-third of blacks are now middle or upper middle class. Another third seem to be a permanent underclass. Never in history has either class been as large as it is now.

6-14 The main division is between those who support greater integration into the mainstream of American society and those who advocate segregation or a revived form of communalism. Groups with many different motivations support the communalistic approach. Some, like Farrakhan's Black Muslims, view contact with whites as corruptive and inherently damaging to blacks. Others, like many black conservatives and academics, view communalism as the only way to revive inner-city neighborhoods and improve the lives of the disadvantaged. For this group, integration does not seem to be a realistic solution. Still others among the cultural elite view communalism as the only way to sustain a vigorous and distinct black culture and social life.

▲ Kwanzaa is an African-American spiritual celebration focusing on the unity of black families and honoring the heritage of the African-American culture. Started by Dr. Maulana Ron Karenga in 1966, the holiday begins on December 26th and lasts seven days. The last day of Kwanzaa is commemorated with a large feast, music, and dancing.

Cultural Subgroups

6-15 The North, the Chesapeake Bay area, and the deep South.

6-16 The large scale movement of southern blacks to northern cities blurred these differences. Other factors that contributed to blurring these differences include: the rise in the education level of the entire population, the civil rights movement, and the increased integration of African Americans into the broader society.

6-17 Africans who came to America as slaves were a very diverse group. They came from different tribes, regions, and religions and spoke different languages. During the years before emancipation, blacks were largely illiterate and divided from each other by slavery and geography. Among the literate, urban black population of this century a new culture, which reflects a common black American consciousness and identity created from 250 years of shared experience in America, has evolved.

6-18 The links are quite weak. Traditional African culture among American blacks largely disappeared under slavery and with the passage of time. Today some people are attempting to reintroduce elements of African culture to the black community. Whether these ideas will endure and become a lasting part of American black culture remains to be seen.

6-19 Kwanzaa celebrates the African roots of black Americans and emphasizes seven basic values that its founder felt should be reinforced in black communities: unity, self-determination, collective work and responsibility, cooperative economics, purpose, creativity, and faith.

6-20 Professor Ron Karenga invented this holiday in 1966 in California. It is a nonsectarian holiday that is meant to reconnect African Americans with some of the values that he felt have been lost in the black community.

6-21 James Weldon Johnson, Marcus Garvey, Roy Innes, Malcolm X, Stokely Carmichael, and Colin Powell.

6-22 Blacks constituted over 90 percent of the population of the British-held islands during the early 20th century. British colonial rulers were forced to educate and train a sizable group of blacks to help administer government offices and fill many positions in the local economy. The variety and scope of economic roles that blacks played in the West Indies was much greater than those of American blacks during the same period. In 1970 over half of the black-owned business in New York City were run by natives of the British West Indies who had immigrated to the United States.

7 CULTURAL LIFE

Music

7-1   The cakewalk and the Charleston.

7-2   Jazz, ragtime, spirituals, gospel, rhythm-and-blues, soul, and rap.

7-3   The entire score of the popular movie *The Sting* was composed of ragtime music. When this movie came out in 1973, it revived interest in ragtime.

7-4   Scott Joplin.

7-5   Ragtime was a form of music that combined folk tunes, African rhythms, and Creole influences. It was played by small groups on the streets of New Orleans and on showboats on the Mississippi River. Joplin studied classical piano in Missouri and lived in St. Louis, where he came into contact with ragtime. He later wrote an instruction book on the musical patterns of ragtime.

7-6   Ragtime, blues, and Dixieland.

7-7   Charlie Parker, Dizzy Gillespie, John Coltrane, Thelonious Monk, and Miles Davis.

7-8   William "Count" Basie led a group of musicians that were considered one of the premier jazz and swing bands of the Big Band era. In 1969 a version of the song "Fly Me to The Moon" recorded by Count Basie and his Orchestra became the first song played on the moon by the Apollo 11 astronauts.

7-9 Ellis, the father of the Marsalis family, is a modern jazz pianist; son Wynton plays jazz and classical trumpet; son Branford plays jazz saxophone, and son Delfeayo is a musical producer.

7-10 Chuck Berry and Little Richard (Richard Penniman).

7-11 In the 1960s, Motown produced a large number of groups that were popular among both blacks and whites. These groups were known for producing a distinctive style of music known as soul.

7-12 Diana Ross and the Supremes; the Jackson Five; Stevie Wonder; Marvin Gaye; the Temptations; Smokey Robinson and the Miracles.

7-13 Aretha Franklin combined the sound of black gospel music with mainstream pop.

7-14 Classical opera.

7-15 Reggae is a form of music created from Caribbean rhythms and American soul music. It originated in Jamaica in the mid-1960s and was introduced to America by Jamaican immigrants and the popular group Bob Marley and the Wailers.

Writers

7-16 Phyllis Wheatley (1753–83) is considered the first American black writer. She was taken from Africa as a slave. At a time when very few blacks were literate, she learned to write literary English as well as Latin. She was known for her poetry and essays.

7-17 Paul Lawrence Dunbar (1872–1906) wrote poetry about black life in America in the dialect of the time. Although he wrote in standard English as well, the dialectic poetry is what he became best known for.

7-18 Important black writers include James Baldwin, Richard Wright, Zora Neale Hurston, Ralph Ellison, Alice Walker, Toni Morrison, and Maya Angelou.

7-19 *Ebony, Jet,* and the *Amsterdam News.*

7-20 Paul Robeson.

7-21 The Harlem Renaissance.

7-22 They wanted to show that black writers could write about universal themes for a general audience, not just for a black audience. They also wanted to present a varied and realistic portrayal of black characters—not just the stock caricatures of obsequious or unruly blacks that appeared in most of the contemporary literature of the time.

7-23 He was the advocate, chronicler, and historian of this renaissance. In his autobiography *Along This Way* (1933), he describes Harlem of the 1920s: "This was the era in which was achieved the Harlem of story and song; the era in which Harlem's fame for exotic flavor and colorful sensuousness was spread to all parts of the world; when Harlem was made known as . . . the center of the new Negro literature and art."

7-24 Langston Hughes.

7-25 The poem "Harlem," which begins with these words: "What happens to a dream deferred? Does it dry up like a raisin in the sun?"

7-26 Lorraine Hansberry wrote this play in 1965. She was a

▲ Langston Hughes was a writer and poet who became popular during, and had a significant effect on, the Harlem Renaissance, a cultural movement among African Americans in the 1920s. His writing was considered to be a realistic depiction of black American life.

very gifted black writer who died at a young age.

7-27 Richard Wright and James Baldwin. Wright in his work *Native Son* (1940) and Baldwin in his most celebrated novels, *Go Tell it on the Mountain* (1953) and *The Fire Next Time* (1963), wrote about the seamier and despairing side of urban black life, unlike the writers of the Harlem Renaissance, who gave a more romanticized portrayal. Wright and Baldwin also wrote from the perspective of being alienated from American society. Both of them spent many years living in Paris.

7-28 *Roots* traces the history of an African slave from his capture in Africa, to his life on a plantation, to the lives of his descendants.

7-29 Many people became interested in investigating the roots of their families, and many blacks became interested in their cultural roots in Africa.

7-30 Maya Angelou, Toni Morrison, Alice Walker, and Gwendolyn Brooks are among the best known African-American women writers.

7-31 This line comes from Paul Lawrence Dunbar's poem "Sympathy."

7-32 Maya Angelou wrote her autobiography in 1970 and took this title from Dunbar's poem.

Comedy, Dance, and Fashion

7-33 Dick Gregory, who also launched a failed presidential bid.

7-34 *Amos 'n' Andy.*

7-35 Ailey sought to reach a mass audience by blending ballet and modern dance and by incorporating black music and dance patterns among other elements.

7-36 He became the first black to dance for the New York City ballet. In 1969 he founded the Harlem Dance Theatre, which is an all-black troupe that performs classical dance.

7-37 The Dashiki was worn as a symbol of the connection between black Americans and their African roots.

7-38 The Afro.

7-39 The style of wearing hair in dreadlocks comes from the island of Jamaica and is associated with the Rastafarian religion.

Intellectual Life

7-40 During the tumultuous 1960s, many black students and white radicals demanded changes in the traditional curriculum of the universities. One of their demands was a curriculum that was "more relevant" to the changing composition of the student body. Black students claimed that black history and culture had been neglected or treated disrespectfully in the traditional curriculum, and that the creation of black studies programs would help correct this problem.

7-41 While some of these programs, such as those at Harvard University and Temple University, are considered scholarly departments, others are not. Some departments, critics charge, have been led by politicized ideologues (e.g., Leonard Jeffries at CCNY in New York) who use their positions to promote their own prejudices and ideologies about black racial superiority.

7-42 Thomas Sowell, Glenn Loury, Clarence Thomas, Alan Keyes, and Shelby Steele.

7-43 Black intellectuals believe that government aid programs do more to foster dependency and prevent strong family formation than to help people get out of poverty. They think that such programs encourage a decline in family values and community institutions, which they believe need to be strengthened in order to eliminate poverty.

7-44 The intellectuals claim that the civil rights leadership is promoting policies that are either outdated (affirmative action-style quotas) or destructive (welfare plans that discourage marriage and work). They criticize the emphasis of the traditional leadership on looking to the government for aid rather than strengthening the trend toward self-help and self-reliance within the black community.

▲ Controversial film director Spike Lee is known for vividly and accurately portraying African Americans and their families in today's society, as well as for his historical pieces. His film adaptation of the life of Malcolm X was the first epic motion picture ever made about a black historical figure, and his hits such as *Jungle Fever* and *Do the Right Thing* have established him as one of the foremost directors in Hollywood.

Film and Television

7-45 Hattie McDaniel played the endearing black mammy (combination nanny and household servant) who gave common-sense advice to her master's wife and daughters, while enduring their foolish behavior with unlimited patience.

7-46 Sidney Poitier appeared in many acclaimed movies: *Something of Value, A Raisin in the Sun, Guess Who's Coming to Dinner,* and *To Sir With Love,* among others.

7-47 Spike Lee has directed many movies, including *She's Gotta Have It, Do the Right Thing, Mo' Better Blues, Jungle Fever,* and *Malcolm X.*

7-48 Bill Cosby starred in a show about the Huxtable family. This show was unique when it was first broadcast (1980s) because it portrayed a black family in which both parents were professionals. It reached an audience of both whites and blacks.

7-49 Oprah Winfrey.

8 POLITICAL PARTICIPATION

The Abolition Movement and the Civil War

8-1   Many of the nation's founders, including Thomas Jefferson, felt that slavery was incompatible with the principles upon which America was founded. They did not include these sentiments in the Declaration of Independence or the Constitution because they feared southern states wouldn't agree to join the union if they did. Without the involvement of all thirteen states, many leaders feared that the young nation would be reclaimed by England.

8-2   Five thousand black slaves fought on the side of the colonists, mainly in the northern colonial regiments. After the Revolutionary War, these soldier-slaves were given their freedom. In all the northern states, laws were passed immediately after the war abolishing slavery as an institution, partly in response to the contribution of blacks during the war.

8-3   The abolition movement in the North was gaining supporters. The philosophy of freedom that character-ized the American independence movement began to influence the issue of slavery.

8-4   Some southern politicians were afraid that if the blacks continued to increase their numbers faster than the whites, the likelihood of slave insurrections would increase. They were aware of a number of bloody slave revolts taking place in the Caribbean at that time.

8-5 Frederick Douglass was a runaway slave who became a great orator and writer for the abolitionist cause. William Wells Brown was another runaway slave who became a writer and speaker for the cause. He wrote the first novel and play by a black person in America.

8-6 *Uncle Tom's Cabin,* written by Harriet Beecher Stowe in 1851, was a story about a black slave and his life in the South.

8-7 The Republican Party was created to oppose the spread of slavery into new territories as the United States continued to expand its borders.

8-8 By the 1890s, the Jim Crow laws of the South had ended black participation in political life altogether. By then, the Republican Party had given up on solving the racial problems of the South.

8-9 Dred Scott and his wife, both slaves, were brought to a free state by their master and then taken back to the South. The Scotts sued their master for their freedom on the grounds that while living on free soil they had become free people. The Supreme Court disagreed by stating that the Scotts were not citizens and therefore had no right to sue.

8-10 Lincoln initially proclaimed that the Civil War was being fought to preserve the union and not primarily to eradicate slavery. He described his goals this way in order not to antagonize people in the southern and border states who supported slavery but wanted to stay in the union. Many northerners were also afraid that a sudden emancipation of the slaves would produce an influx of southern blacks into northern cities and change labor markets and housing patterns.

8-11 Roughly 180,000 black soldiers saw service in the Union army. They made up about 10 percent of its soldiers.

Reconstruction and Northern Politics

8-12 The 13th Amendment, abolishing slavery, went into effect in 1865; the 14th Amendment, guaranteeing equal rights for all citizens except Native Americans, went into effect in 1868; the 15th Amendment, guaranteeing the right to vote for all male citizens regardless of race, went into effect in 1870; and the 19th Amendment, giving the right to vote to all women, went into effect in 1920.

8-13 Immediately after the Civil War, discriminatory laws called "Black Codes" were put in place. By the end of the century, a pervasive system of "Jim Crow" laws were enacted by most southern states. These laws kept blacks from voting and legally segregated them.

8-14 In 1967, Andrew Young became the next black person to be elected to Congress from the South, after the passage of the National Voting Rights Act in 1965.

8-15 Blacks enthusiastically supported both the election of Franklin D. Roosevelt as president and the beginning of the New Deal.

8-16 The association of the Republican Party with emancipation drove the great bulk of southern whites into the arms of the Democratic Party. The white southern vote was overwhelmingly Democratic until the 1960s, when the Democratic Party supported the civil rights movement. This support led many southern whites to turn to the Republican Party.

8-17 Adolph Plessy was a black man (he was only one-eighth black by ancestry) who sued when he was told he had to travel in a railway car reserved for blacks only. The Supreme Court upheld the claim of the train line that racial segregation was acceptable if it provided "separate but equal" treatment for both races.

8-18 This decision provided the rationale for creating segregated institutions of all types (schools, theaters, buses) under the cover of claiming that the services were separate but equal.

▼ Until the civil rights movement in the 1960s, unfair laws, called "Jim Crow" laws after a popular minstrel character of the 1820s that demeaned blacks, allowed legal discrimination against African Americans, who were forced to use separate facilities such as water fountains and public restrooms, and sit in all-black sections of buses, theaters, and restaurants.

8-19 Ida Wells campaigned fearlessly against lynching and racial violence. Due to such efforts, anti-lynching laws were passed.

8-20 Blanche K. Bruce was elected in 1874 in Mississippi.

8-21 Edward Brooke, a Republican from Massachusetts, was elected in 1966—almost a full century after the previous black senator.

8-22 The black clergy and middle class were mostly conservative in their social views and were not inclined to support utopian, atheistic ideologies. Poor African Americans didn't find communism credible as an ideology since it viewed class conflict as the main cause of poverty, not race. The poor blacks saw race as being an important factor in their lives, and a main cause of their poverty. They also were suspicious of white communists, whom they saw as agitators looking to use blacks to advance their political ambitions.

8-23 W. E. B. DuBois, A. Philip Randolph, and Paul Robeson.

8-24 He was an apologist for Stalinist Russia and never recanted his views, even after the truth about Stalin's deeds became known.

The Civil Rights Era

8-25 *Brown v. The Board of Education* was a challenge to the legalized segregation of public schools. The Supreme Court declared that legal segregation was unconstitutional. It reasoned that separate schools, under the conditions of those times, produced inherently unequal conditions for learning.

8-26 "The Movement" referred to the sit-ins and protests against legalized discrimination and segregation in the South.

8-27 The Congress on Racial Equality established in 1942 and the Southern Christian Leadership Conference established in 1957 fought for civil rights.

8-28 A black woman named Rosa Parks sat down in the front section of a bus. Those seats were reserved for whites. When a white man entered the bus and asked her to move, she refused and was arrested. This sparked a year-long boycott of the bus line until the Supreme Court declared segregated seating unconstitutional.

8-29 Dr. King drew upon the idea of civil disobedience put forth by Henry David Thoreau and the theory of nonviolent resistance advocated by Mahatma Gandhi. He used these concepts to pressure white political and business leaders to grant equal treatment for blacks.

8-30 In the first case, Little Rock Central High School was integrated in spite of opposition from much of the white population. In the second case, the University of Alabama was integrated.

8-31 In 1963, a March on Washington for Freedom and Jobs was organized by civil rights groups. Two hundred thousand people participated in this march, both black and white.

8-32 The 100th anniversary of the signing of the Emancipation Proclamation by President Lincoln took place in 1963. Even after 100 years of nominal freedom, African Americans still didn't have equal rights of citizenship.

8-33 America in the 1960s was involved in a cold war with the Soviet Union. Each side tried to win support from recently decolonized countries of the Third World. Many American political leaders felt that they couldn't appeal for support from these countries and play the

▲ The men of Company E, 4th U.S. Colored Infantry, stand at parade rest in 1865. Although they faced discrimination at nearly every turn, the African-American soldiers of the Civil War were fighting for more than their country—they were fighting for their freedom. By the end of the war, over 180,000 African Americans had fought in the U.S. military.

role of leader of the free world as long as nonwhites in America were not being treated as well as whites.

8-34 Successful lawsuits brought by the NAACP; a major change in the attitude of whites toward blacks since World War II; a willingness on the part of Congress, the president, and the Supreme Court to pass and enforce laws protecting civil rights for blacks; and successful tactics by black leaders in using demonstrations and sit-ins while maintaining standards of nonviolent behavior.

8-35 Whites at all economic levels, but particularly at the lower levels, did not feel as threatened by black competition and advancement when economic opportunities were growing.

8-36 By the end of the Civil War (1865), the South was economically in ruins. A large portion of the male population had been killed or wounded in the war. Moreover, the defeat by the North was a great humiliation to proud southerners, and it was made worse by the cynical and opportunistic behavior of northern carpetbaggers. Under these conditions, white southerners were not in a mood to grant equality to freed slaves. In contrast, the 1950s and early '60s was a period of peace and growing prosperity for the white South.

8-37 Many blacks who were interested in running for political office had a chance to do so. During this period, black leaders were able to encourage a large number of African American adults to register and vote. Since the Voting Rights Act concentrated many African Americans in the same electoral districts, black candidates were able to carry the vote. Also, more whites were willing to vote for black candidates.

8-38 Many advocates of Black Power (Stokely Carmichael and H. Rap Brown, for example) had argued that the nonviolent tactics of Dr. King and others would not produce lasting results. Dr. King's assassination temporarily seemed to vindicate them.

8-39 These movements radicalized them and encouraged an attitude of challenging established authority. This change undermined black churches and their middle-class leadership in the inner cities.

8-40 Rustin was an advocate of integration and nonviolent protest. Even when many other figures in the movement (e.g., Jesse Jackson and Stokely Carmichael) took a more confrontational pose and began to advocate a uniracial black power approach, Rustin never changed his views that blacks could advance in America only with the cooperation of whites. As the more radical advocates gained popularity and visibility, Bayard Rustin faded from public view.

The Post-Civil Rights Era

8-41 Opponents quickly reconciled themselves to the equalization of blacks in public life. Political figures such as George Wallace who had launched careers by using race-baiting tactics in the 1950s began courting and successfully winning black votes in elections of the 1970s and '80s.

8-42 The Rev. Jesse Jackson sought to capitalize on his strong showing in the presidential primaries of 1984 and 1988 by forming a political coalition of groups that in his view had traditionally been shut out of power: blacks, Hispanics, Asians, women, and homosexuals.

8-43 The Rainbow Coalition had largely faded away by the 1990s. The different parts of this coalition had conflicting agendas. Many people began to see the organization as a vehicle for the self-promotion of its leaders rather than as a cooperative political alliance.

8-44 They are Republicans with conservative views who were elected in districts that are mostly white. These black politicians won by taking stands on issues and by producing results for a diverse electorate. They didn't position themselves as representatives of the "black vote."

8-45 From the 1950s through the 1980s, black politicians were elected by solid black majorities in highly segregated districts or by coalitions of blacks and liberal whites. As the population becomes more diverse and African Americans become more dispersed, black politicians will have to make coalitions with many different groups within the population and develop a broader base of support.

8-46 Nelson Mandela.

8-47 Generally blacks have not taken an active interest in African affairs. The one exception to this was the anti-apartheid struggle in South Africa. Since South African blacks now have political power, this cause is no longer as relevant.

9 IMPORTANT PERSONALITIES and PEOPLE OF ACCOMPLISHMENT

▲ Father and son Benjamin O. Davis Sr. and Benjamin O. Davis Jr. each broke barriers in the U.S. military. In 1940 Benjamin Davis Sr. (right) became the first African-American general in the U.S. Army. During World War II, he helped develop the first major change in the army's policy of segregating black and white troops by assigning 5,000 African-American infantry replacements to previously all-white regiments. In 1936, Benjamin Davis Jr. (left) became the first black man to graduate from West Point Military Academy in over 50 years. He served in World War II as a fighter pilot and squadron commander, and later became the first black general of the United States Air Force.

Intellectual and Cultural Figures

9-1 Benjamin Banneker (1731–1806).

9-2 Carver is known for introducing crop rotation into the one-crop South and inventing many synthetic products from peanuts and soybeans.

9-3 Lewis Latimer (1848–1928).

9-4 McCoy invented various types of automatic lubricating machines for engines. His inventions were widely imitated. The expression "the real McCoy" is believed to come from his name, referring to something of the highest quality and authenticity.

9-5 Mary MacLeod Bethune founded a school in Florida for black children. It became Bethune College in 1923. President Roosevelt appointed her an adviser on Negro affairs for the National Youth Administration.

9-6 The Daughters of the American Revolution (DAR) refused to let Marian Anderson sing in Constitution Hall in 1939. Eleanor Roosevelt resigned from the DAR, and the Secretary of the Interior invited Anderson to sing on the steps of the Lincoln Memorial.

9-7 Derek Wolcott.

Elected and Appointed Public Figures

9-8 Bunche won the prize for his work to peacefully resolve the Arab-Israeli war in 1948–49.

9-9 Thurgood Marshall was appointed by President Lyndon B. Johnson in 1967.

9-10 Harlem.

9-11 Unlike most other black mayors, Bradley was elected by an electorate that was overwhelmingly white.

9-12 David Dinkins was elected in 1989.

9-13 Clarence Thomas was appointed by President Bush in 1991.

Sports

9-14 Jackie Robinson began playing for the Brooklyn Dodgers in 1947.

9-15 Joe Louis.

9-16 Cassius Clay (Muhammad Ali).

9-17 Adolf Hitler wanted to use the Berlin Olympics as a showcase for the superiority of Aryan and German athletes. The victories by Owens and other black athletes embarrassed Hitler to the extent that he refused to shake hands with them. The Olympic committee then told Hitler that he had to shake hands with all of the athletes or none of them. He decided to shake no one's hand.

9-18 Wilma Rudolph.

9-19 About 80 percent.

9-20 Arthur Ashe won the U.S. Open in 1968; the Australian Open in 1970; and Wimbledon in 1975.

9-21 Althea Gibson won both tennis titles in 1957 and 1958.

9-22 Henry Aaron, hit 755 home runs, surpassing Ruth's record of 714, which was once considered unbreakable.

▲ The legendary Jesse Owens broke many track and field records at the 1936 Olympic games held in Berlin. He won gold medals in four events: the 100-meter dash, 200-meter dash, long jump, and the 400-meter team relay. Ironically, Owens's display of speed and skill came before an audience that had been told by German leader Adolf Hitler that the Berlin Olympics would be a showcase for "Aryan supremacy."

Military Service

9-23 General Benjamin O. Davis Sr. was promoted in 1940, one year before America entered World War II.

9-24 Colin Powell was appointed chairman of the Joint Chiefs in 1989.

Further Reading

D'Souza, Dinesh. "We the Slaveholders," *Policy Review* 74: 30-38 (Fall 1995).

Fage, J. D. *A History of Africa*. London: Routledge, 1995.

Farley, Reynolds. Blacks and Whites: *Narrowing the Gap?* Cambridge: Harvard University Press, 1984.

Franklin, John Hope, and Alfred A. Moss Jr. *From Slavery to Freedom: A History of African Americans*. MacGraw Hill, 1987.

Gates, Henry Louis Jr., and Cornell West. *The Future of the Race*. New York: Alfred A. Knopf, 1996.

Quarles, Benjamin. *The Negro in the Making of America*. New York: MacMillan, 1987.

Raboteau, Albert J. *A Fire in the Bones*. Boston: Beacon Press, 1995.

Smead, Howard. *The Afro-Americans*. New York: Chelsea House, 1989.

Sowell, Thomas. *The Economics and Politics of Race*. New York: William Morrow, 1983.

Sowell, Thomas. *Race and Culture: A World View*. New York: Basic Books, 1994.

Thernstrom, Stephan, Ann Orlov, and Oscar Handlin (editors). *The Harvard Ethnic Encyclopedia of America*. Cambridge, Massachusetts: The Belknap Press, 1980.

Thernstrom, Stephan, and Abigail Thernstrom. *America in Black and White*. New York: Simon and Schuster, 1997.

Index

Index

Index

Picture Credits

About the Contributors

General Editor SANDRA STOTSKY is director of the Institute on Writing, Reading, and Civic Education at the Harvard Graduate School of Education as well as a research associate there. She served as editor of *Research in the Teaching of English,* a journal sponsored by the National Council of Teachers of English, from 1991–97.

Dr. Stotsky holds a bachelor of arts degree with distinction from the University of Michigan and a doctorate in education from the Harvard Graduate School of Education. She has taught on the elementary and high school levels and at Northeastern University, Curry College, and the Harvard Graduate School of Education. Her work in education has ranged from serving on academic advisory boards to developing elementary and secondary civics curricula as a consultant to American, Polish, Lithuanian and Romanian educators. She has written numerous scholarly articles, curricular materials, encyclopedia entries, and reviews, and is the author of three books on education.

General Editor REED UEDA is associate professor of history at Tufts University. He graduated summa cum laude with a bachelor of arts degree from UCLA, received master of arts degrees from both the University of Chicago and Harvard University, and received a doctorate from Harvard.

Dr. Ueda was research editor of the *Harvard Ethnic Encyclopedia of America* and has served on the board of editors for *American Quarterly, Harvard Educational Review, Journal of Interdisciplinary History,* and *University of Chicago School Review.* He is the author or coauthor of several books on ethnic studies, including *Postwar Immigrant America: A Social History, Ethnic Groups in History Textbooks,* and *Immigration.*

ELLEN SHNIDMAN has written articles and essays on social issues for a number of journals. She has also coauthored articles on the social and biological sciences. She graduated magna cum laude from Yale University and earned a master of science degree from the Weizmann Institute of Science in Israel. She lives in Rochester, New York.